THE EURO IN DANGER

First published 2012 by Searching Finance Ltd, 200 Queen Edith's Way, Cambridge CB1 8NL, UK

ISBN: 978-1-907720-63-5

Typeset and designed by Deirdré Gyenes

THE EURO IN DANGER

REFORM AND RESET

Jagjit S Chadha

Michael A H Dempster

Derry Pickford

S⦾arching finance

Authors' note

This book draws on conversations and work undertaken by the authors from December 2011 to September 2012. The opinions expressed here are those of the authors and not necessarily those of the institutions with which they are affiliated.

About the authors

JAGJIT S. CHADHA: Professor of Economics, Chair in Banking and Finance, University of Kent, and CIMF, Cambridge.
E-mail: jsc@kent.ac.uk.

MICHAEL A H DEMPSTER: Professor Emeritus, Centre for Financial Research, Department of Pure Mathematics and Statistics, University of Cambridge and Cambridge Systems Associates Limited.
E-mail: mahd2@cam.ac.uk

DERRY E PICKFORD: Macro-Analyst, Ashburton London, a division of FirstRand Bank Limited (London Branch).
E-mail: derry.pickford@ashburton.com

For full author biographies, see page 87

About Searching Finance

Searching Finance publishes and curates economics, finance and politics.
Follow us on Facebook at www.facebook.com/searchingfinance
Our website is: www.searchingfinance.com

PREFACE

WE WROTE this book as the result of a number of passionate, and it must be admitted heated, conversations on the EMU question before Christmas 2011, around the time of the Fiscal Compact, which led to a first draft in January this year. We are putting the finishing touches to the work on the 20th anniversary of the UK's exit from the ERM, which occurred on 16th September 1992. European events continue to dominate the UK agenda, but now also the sentiment in global financial markets. We each have grown up with the spectre of the European question: How far should the UK integrate into the European project? The answer to that question has continually provided the context for so much of the UK policy agenda that it has sometimes proved hard to think more profoundly about the question in the Kennedy sense of not what the Euro can do for us but what we can do for the Euro. Undoubtedly, the missing ingredient in the Euro debate is what we might call good old-fashioned market liberalism. That would probably have been the main contribution that UK entry to EMU could have provided to Euro policy-making elite. We maintain in what follows that financial markets are not to be feared but, as they are enormously powerful machines for processing information, to be learnt from. However, they must also be intelligently managed, as they are prone to fads and fashions. We have tried here to collect up a number of such observations and comments into an agenda for reform in terms of necessary steps towards a functional Eurozone. This is not because we think that common currency ought to fail, but because we think that the current situation can and should be rescued. However, time is short. Already the sinews of the policymakers have been stretched to breaking point, and sadly, economic and monetary policy is not far behind.

JSC, MAHD & DEP
CAMBRIDGE & LONDON, 16TH SEPTEMBER 2012

PREFACE

CONTENTS

Summary ix

1. Introduction 1
   1.1 Context of European monetary dislocation 1
   1.2 The basic issue 5
   1.3 The growing crisis 8

2. Economic and Monetary Union: A Pyrrhic Victory 15
   2.1 Problems, problems 15
   2.2 Failure of the 2011/12 reforms to date 21

3. Institution Building 29
   3.1 European Central Bank reforms 29
   3.2 European financial system regulation 36
   3.3 European derivative legislation 41
   3.4 European Sovereign Fiscal Council establishment 51
   3.5 European Sovereign Bankruptcy Court establishment 53
   3.6 Summary of recommendations 54

4. Monetary Arrangements 57
   4.1 Late 20th century solutions to credible commitment 57
   4.2 Escape routes and exit clauses 58
   4.3 Historical currency unions and break-ups 59
   4.4 Eurozone break-up issues 73
   4.5 The reset option 74
   4.6 Introducing a new currency 78

5. Conclusion 79

Bibliography 81

Authors' Biographies 87

SUMMARY

IN THIS BOOK we outline a set of measures that are urgently required for the resolution of the Eurozone's chronic existential crisis. The recent thrust of many solutions has been Euro-sceptic, while the pronouncements of leading politicians – although largely upbeat about the prospects for the Euro – continue to be rather vague. We actually want the Euro to succeed and flourish, but looking at the current and likely configuration of policy, institutions and economic structure we remain gravely concerned.

We argue that the crisis results from five distinct pressures on the system:

(i)   Institutional arrangements for EMU that address inflation risk but deal inadequately with default risk;

(ii) Prolonged procrastination about a serious recapitalisation of the entire Eurozone banking system;

(iii) Escalating levels of intra-union claims held to a significant degree by these same highly leveraged financial institutions;

(iv) Absence of a fiscal mechanism that forces the recycling of claims from creditors back to debtors; and

(v)   Lack of sufficient internal price and wage flexibility in a significant rump of countries.

These pressures have led to unsustainable debt levels in a number of EMU member countries, in particular, Greece.

A single central bank standing at the centre of this system cannot set policy to offset the structural imbalances in payments, as monetary policy can essentially only facilitate rather than ensure real adjustment. Furthermore, as long as the required scale of fiscal transfers is ruled out politically and while an accompanying requirement for the consolidation of the EMU banking system is only currently under debate, the Eurozone remains highly vulnerable to stagnation and decomposition. We therefore suggest a new set of collective policy options for EMU member states which would take the European project to the next, rather than ultimate, level of integration more safely than the current muddle-through.

At the centre of our recommendations is the development of a new option for EMU member states facing chronic payments problems which we call the *reset option*. Under the reset option a member state with a significant payments problem can temporarily leave the monetary union, but remain a member of the EU. Rather than the opt-out exercised by the UK and Denmark, the reset option allows a country to leave with an ongoing objective of returning at some future point. Rather than simply facing the options of continuing with unsustainable sovereign debt levels or being ejected from EMU with an uncertain monetary future, the reset option will comprise the following actions of the nation exercising the new option:

- Once assessed as having unsustainable debt levels by a newly created Fiscal Council, a country such as Greece will have the option to seek the reset option via a newly established Sovereign Bankruptcy Court;

- Leave the Eurozone and the direct jurisdiction of the ECB and create a new domestic currency, which will allow an external devaluation versus the Euro and thereby allow competitiveness to be restored in the traditional manner;

- Create a nominal anchor by a crawling peg with wide bands against the Euro;

- Fund the balance of payments with a sequence of IMF programmes;

- Accept heightened monitoring of fiscal policy by a new EMU Fiscal Council;

- Negotiate a haircut of sovereign debt through the new Sovereign Bankruptcy Court;

- Set high reserve and capital requirements for the operations of the domestic banking system, to be reduced to EMU levels upon the expiry of the option;

- Pass annual Acts of Parliament that commit the nation to a return to the Euro at some point in the future, at a reasonable exchange rate to be agreed in advance.

The current process of alleviating structural payments problems seems much more ad hoc than the development of a specific option. Essentially, to date countries have sought IMF balance of payments assistance, implemented fiscal reform packages alongside some structural reform and received some voluntary debt forgiveness. The ECB has provided large quantities of short-term liquidity, but sovereign risks have not been especially alleviated and this is because these policies do little to promote expectations of sustained growth in nominal GDP. The latest bond-buying programme does not help eliminate structural payments problems; it simply provides a temporary panacea for excessive debt issuance.

As well as creating the reset option open to all EMU member states, the members of the monetary union remaining will have to accept reforms which will strengthen the system. A number of principal-agent problems can be solved with institution building rather than a further expansion in the powers of the European Commission, per se. These include:

- The development of an *independent* Fiscal Council to monitor and report on all member states' fiscal plans, both in terms of their national solvency and with respect to the union's payments position;

- The creation of a European Stability Mechanism with funding not only from members of EMU but also multilateral funding through the IMF, with support from within the EU and its key trading partners, with more capital funding supplied by the highly-rated EU nations;

- A new market-oriented set of financial system and derivative regulations and some intermediate steps towards a banking union to include Euro deposit insurance;

- The clear commitment of the ECB to act as a lender of last resort (in the Bagehot sense) for all members of Stage 3 of EMU and to stand at the centre of the TARGET 2 payment system with sufficient capital, with operations to be conducted *only* in the secondary markets for debt and *no* monetary financing of national deficits.

The costs to a nation utilising the reset option militate against any great moral hazard issues arising from its exercise. We believe that carrying out the suggested reforms in parallel with developing the reset option will provide the best way of ensuring the future growth and prosperity of the full current membership of EMU. Developing the reset will not only facilitate structural economic reform and enable states to retire formally debt that is excessive, but will also provide a formal mechanism for the resolution of payments problems based on orderly negotiations.

We do not claim that the reset option is a panacea. Its aim is *not* to make breaks from the Eurozone an attractive option, but rather to provide an alternative to disorderly exits with the enormous associated costs involved. We argue that a corollary of reset is tighter rules on bank capital and macro-prudential regulation, over and above what is already envisaged. However, by removing the enormous legal uncertainty and the likelihood of excessive exchange rate volatility arising from uncoordinated exits, we hope that market participants will be able to better judge ex ante the probability of redenomination. And so will reduce the level of uncertainty which is currently impacting economic activity, not only in the periphery of the Eurozone but in the global economy.

CHAPTER 1

INTRODUCTION

1.1 Context of European monetary dislocation

THE EUROPEAN ECONOMIC AND MONETARY UNION (EMU) is in a state of chronic existential crisis. The long sweep of monetary history is littered with many failed regimes and there is now a real danger that EMU will follow its predecessors into collapse. The failure of monetary regimes, as with all complex events, cannot be ascribed to any single cause. But it is clear that many of the ideas about how to run a monetary regime have been ignored in the first incarnation of EMU: the monetary and fiscal institutions are hampered by insufficient firepower and the economic region encompassed by EMU is itself far from an optimum currency area. However, a careful reading of the factors that have contributed to this crisis suggests that there is a way to escape. But time is short, and both political and economic decision-making has been sclerotic in the face of the growing crisis. In this book we propose a number of reforms to the existing international monetary and fiscal settlement aimed at the survival of EMU in order to enable the development of an option to allow some nations to exit EMU, but remain in the EU. We call this the *reset option*. Alongside the new option we propose a number of reforms to the EMU monetary-fiscal constellation.

EMU was launched in the middle of the longest economic expansion of the post-war period, which serendipitously masked many of the emerging economic problems. Even in countries experiencing different economic shocks, living standards can rise in lockstep during an expansion, despite differential productivity growth rates, because of easy access to money. In fact, some of this tendency to grow together constitutes the risk sharing which was supposed to be the great feature of a monetary union. The ongoing financial crisis has, however, ruthlessly exposed the weaknesses of the current monetary union. These weaknesses stem ultimately from a lack of real convergence across member countries, that has been exacerbated by a lack of sufficient downward price and wage flexibility. The financial sector, which has been recycling funds from both within the Eurozone and without, has become more and more unstable as the probability of some form of default on intra-union claims has become increasingly likely. This instability stems in turn from the refusal until recently of virtually all EMU nations to recognise the true impact of the subprime crisis on their under-capitalised banks, both global and national. In this context, a banking union appears to us secondary to proper recapitalisation of banks and the consideration of appropriate macro-prudential rules for individual bank behaviour. Nevertheless, banking consolidation can help to provide an enhanced private sector channel for capital transfer complementary to inter-governmental fiscal transfers.

Fiscal policy has not been able to effect a sufficient degree of transfer to offset differential growth rates and, in any case, for many individual states, bond spreads seem to be telling us that this particular arm of policy is nearly exhausted. Monetary policy, after some early successes with liquidity provision in 2007, has been insufficiently accommodative. The recent announcement of a bond-buying programme for indebted states only provides a temporary palliative, as the debt will continue to be excessive without sustained growth.

All this means that states with low growth have ended the economic cycle with high levels of debt and a limited ability repay. This excess debt is the key hurdle which any solution to the Eurozone crisis must overcome.

We can learn some lessons from the post-war experience. Under the Bretton Woods system of fixed-but-adjustable-exchange rates, there were no financial crises to speak of (other than in Brazil in 1962), but also there were considerable controls on capital and credit creation, particularly across borders. More recently, the UK and Italy's dual exit from the European Exchange Rate Mechanism (ERM) and Spain's devaluation in 1992 had a dramatic effect upon these nations and European unity. This event was not unforseen, see Walters (1990). The key adjustment to differential inflation rates in these cases, was to use the exchange rate to regain external competiveness. The problem with this tactic is that it can become a monetary strategy and so lead to a sequence of beggar-thy-neighbour devaluations and the end of the monetary unit of valuation. The real problem, of course, is that we simply do not know on a bilateral basis what the correct or equilibrium exchange rate might be, because the economy is constantly evolving in response to innovation which affects sectoral and aggre-gate demand and supply. Leaving the external valuation of a currency to the markets appears to have injected excessive volatility into exchange rates, but this has reflected, as much as anything else, poor monetary policy that interpreted the economic slowdown in the 1970s as telling us about lower demand rather than about in adequate capacity. The solution seemed to be to tie the hands of politically sensitive monetary policy makers with central bank independence. This solution still makes a great deal of sense from the perspective of real or apparent incentives to inflation, but it actually did very little to deal with the perennial problem of identifying financial bubbles that typically lead to a crisis. It is not so much that monetary policy-makers tried to get things on purpose wrong, but more that they simply do not have enough information to be able to get them all the time right. These informational problems are, of course, exacerbated by poor institutional design. Often following these kinds of ex ante errors, an ex post loosening of monetary conditions is required, and for an open economy a large part of this adjustment is in the exchange rate. The individual members of the Eurozone do not have this facility, either with each other or with the rest of the world. In aggregate the Euro can fluctuate, but that will tend to reflect an average exchange rate impetus across all the economies which is unlikely to be correct for any individual economy.

The experiences of the Latin American debt crisis are also instructive. The recycling of petro-dollars to developing countries from commercial banks after the 1970s oil price shocks, led, after years of financial repression, to unsustainable national debts, or in economists' jargon, debt overhang. Many, in particular Latin American, countries grew external debt denominated in a foreign currency to such a degree that its repayment could not be helped by external exchange rate devaluation. Even though exports might increase, they could never increase enough to meet interest rate and principal repayments, which themselves would be increased in proportion to the scale of any devaluation. The debt, in a phrase borrowed from corporate finance, would *overhang*. Ultimately, in the teeth of much sustained opposition, these debts required orderly restructuring and many of the debtor economies have subsequently found some element of stability. The restructuring required the voluntary restructuring of at least 17 countries' non-performing commercial bank debt into bonds and the rescheduling of 88 countries' medium-term intergovernmental and export credit debt under, respectively, the London and Paris Clubs.

We also think that aspects of the experience of the collapse of communism across the Eastern European states over 1989 to

1991 also yield some helpful points. First, an inflexible approach to divergent economic performance will *ultimately* undermine any monetary unit, whatever the level of dirigisme or control that is ceded to the centre. Secondly, markets to produce, allocate and distribute goods and services do not simply spring into action. Moreover, they require a careful underpinning with legal practice and institutional reform. Thirdly, lagging living standards *cannot* be tolerated for a generation, and therefore viable reforms must not lead to a prolonged downturn in relative performance. Finally, the market price signalling mechanism must be heeded and this implies that domestic prices and exchange rates cannot be set by dictat.

So far the current approach to reform of the Eurozone does not really address the lessons learnt from post-war monetary experience, from the quest for price stability with the genuine lack of full information when setting monetary policy, to the need to allow for external devaluation and debt forgiveness in extremis and the need to recover positive and converging rates of growth in an economic area. The current patchwork of ill co-ordinated policies may at best be described as bumbling and, at worst, a concoction of impotent potions. What we need is a significantly clearer plan for reform.

1.2 The basic issue

The problems in the Eurozone have dominated the economic agenda over the past couple of years. Where the scale of chronic payment problems would seem to imply the need for radical reform, the European leadership has failed to convincingly address institutional arrangements, the payments problems, banking system stability or the sovereign debt crisis. As a result, faltering economic growth has become endemic. The escalation in the level of public debt is the natural consequence of overvalued exchange rates and slow economic growth in many member states of the Eurozone. As public indebtedness reaches its borrowing thresholds, sovereign spreads start to widen, making the debt constraints bite even harder.

Rather than seeking any disbandment of the Eurozone, we advise that considerable and serious attention should be paid to institution building at the European level and that an option to reset needs to be established, so that countries facing domestic and external payments problems could leave the hard Eurozone *temporarily* under the guidance of IMF-style surveillance. As far as we can see, historically all monetary unions that were not also in the first instance a nation state contained some method by which countries could leave. We recommend that the Euro should also have such a formal mechanism as soon as possible.

Naturally, the whole issue of the European sovereign crisis is a matter of political economy, so that, although economists can describe the ideal as a framework, a *practical* solution to the crisis must take account of *political* realities – specifically that complete monetary and fiscal union of the EMU states along the general lines of the US federal union *mutatis mutandis* will not happen soon, or at all ever, without strong leadership. A *fortiori* , we assume here that the current reluctance of EMU nations, jointly or severally, to embody interstate fiscal transfers and pooled sovereign debt in their recently ratified 9th December 2011 agreement and 20th January 2012 Summit and subsequently is an ongoing state of nature. Setting up Eurobonds is fraught with so many well documented difficulties that these bonds, jointly backed by EMU states, must await *full* fiscal union. Fiscal transfers in a full currency union occur both governmentally among and between states and privately through the banking system; both routes are ultimately necessary. On the latter side, it remains to be seen whether or not current efforts to create a Eurozone consolidation of the banking system is politically feasible.

All this means that the prescription of *minimal* requirements for a functioning currency union – a fully functioning central bank, a consolidated banking system, fiscal transfers and labour mobility – of Robert Mundell (1961), who some take to be the father of EMU, still lie far into the future for the Eurozone.

Therefore, currently practical recommendations to address the crisis should be minimal in the sense of being as close to politically feasible as possible, i.e. requiring only feasible negotiations to achieve. To this end:

- EMU sovereigns should attempt to retain the engagement with global financial markets which they have enjoyed over domestic financial markets, but this will require participation in international agreements, including within the EU.

- Sovereigns within EMU should retain responsibility for their own debts, as in Maastricht and Lisbon, which, however, may need to be restructured as circumstances demand.

It may be easier to negotiate changes to the European Central Bank (ECB) directive with the 17 states of the EMU, or to the structure of the European Court of Justice with the 27 states of the EU, than changes to the fiscal disciplines of states, even augmented by some measures for growth. In particular, nearly balanced national budgeting, as currently proposed by France and Germany and incorporated in the EMU 9th December 2011 Agreement and 30th January 2012 EU Summit, is totally impractical without a permanent interstate fiscal transfer mechanism, as occurred early in the formation of the United States (Sheets and Sockin, 2012a). Fiscal positions of EMU states will *always* vary relatively and over time.

As well as a host of institution-building devices, we propose in this book that it will be necessary to design a mechanism to allow a country such as Greece to exit the Euro and yet avoid an ongoing messy default. A nation exiting may even consider continuing to use the Euro as currency as a measure interim to the possible establishment of a new national currency. In making recommendations for setting up new European institutions to address the resulting EMU difficulties and suppress 'contagion', we apply the principle that every opportunity should be taken to improve the *accountability* and *democratic* nature of the new institutions over the status quo. We therefore consider that it is preferable to develop a reset option for any country exiting EMU. Such an option was developed under the Gold Standard and the UK itself exercised this option with a great degree of success from 1797 to 1819 as it struggled with Napoleon's France. In developing a reset option for *temporary* exit of EMU, financial markets will come to recognise the existence of a safety valve and this will allow time for EMU countries to reform their monetary, banking and payment systems. The reset option will be costly for any country to exercise, as it will have heightened monitoring of its fiscal plans, operate monetary policy within a peg with the Euro and suffer greater regulatory controls on its financial services. Therefore the costs of temporary exit will not make this an easy option, but we consider that from a national viewpoint it will be preferable to the slow death of the current policy deadlock and the possibility of a complete monetary fiasco that a disorderly exit might bring about.

1.3 The growing crisis

Over the past year or so, growing tensions within the EMU have threatened the existence not only of the European Union but also of the continuation of the integrated system of world trade and payments. It has become increasingly clear that the EMU, embarked upon in 1999 by 11 countries, and then extended in five staggered steps to 17 by 1st January 2011 with the accession of Estonia, was premature. Not only did the set of countries not constitute an *optimal currency area* (OCA), but there had been insufficient analysis of the problems of running monetary and fiscal policies in a large multi-state monetary union. An OCA is, of course, a set of regions over which there are a sufficiently similar aggregate demand shocks in each region that a single interest rate operating across the regions, subject to individual regions' arrangements over fiscal transfers, is sufficient to allow adjustment to such shocks. The absence of an optimal currency area has meant that shocks, particularly the extreme ones associated with the financial crisis of 2007 onwards, have led to sharply divergent prospects for stable adjustment paths across the Eurozone. It *may* be possible to solve the problem of this premature monetary union without one or more countries leaving, even on a temporary basis. However, we think that this is a highly unlikely outcome, and therefore in this book we outline a way in which a country or group of countries could leave the monetary union and yet secure reasonable prospects for the remaining whole.

Figure 1: Selected Eurozone members' 10-year benchmark yield spreads over Bunds

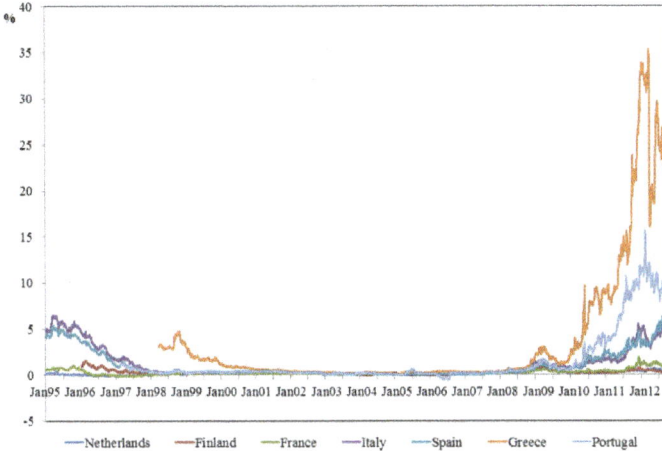

Source: Bloomberg and authors' calculations

In a monetary union, the absence of both synchronised shocks and a similar economic structure means that a unified monetary policy, in the absence of sufficiently flexible wages and prices, will over time and successive business cycles impose *large* welfare losses on many households. In the early stages of EMU this problem was glossed over, leading to the chimera of convergence in long-term interest rates across member countries that were typically treated as indicating the extent to which market participants attached credibility to the monetary union (see Figure 1). Similar charts for 3- and 5-year maturity sovereign bonds are remarkably – and perhaps, in light of text book risk theory, surprisingly – similar.

In fact, these convergent long-term rates reflected other strong forces acting on bond yields at the time: pooled Eurozone money markets that play a key role in determining long-term interest rates, the falling market price of risk during an economic boom, and also a prevailing market view that sovereign states within the monetary union would not be allowed to default, an implicit *guarantee*. Although a monetary union implies a single short-term interest rate for central bank money, and other short-term money market rates, it does not necessarily imply convergence of all market rates across the union, as borrowers can still have idiosyncratic risk – for example, due to differing fiscal policies leading to differing sovereign default risks (Di Cesare *et al.*, 2012) or differing labour costs (see Figure 2). But these factors acted to mask the differences in the required rate of return for such risks and so encouraged the creation of intra- and extra-union claims (see Figure 3). In fact, the convergence of long-term interest rates allowed economies to use debt in order to promote growth even in the absence of productivity increases.

Figure 2: Trend in unit labour costs of Germany and peripheral Eurozone countries

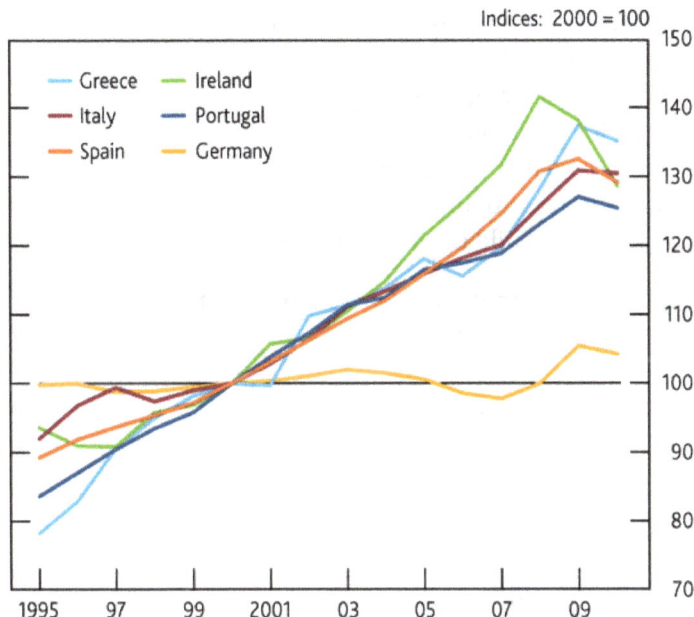

Source: Financial Stability Review, Bank of England, December 2011

So the problem currently faced can also be expressed in the following way. Countries within the monetary union have become increasingly indebted to others in the union. In many cases, the overall level of gross debt is high relative to an individual country's nominal GNP, which threatens sustainability of the debt position. Adjustment thus requires either, or both of, increased saving at the national level and higher growth in nominal GNP. If debtor countries all try to save at the same time there is the danger, because of a lack of co-ordination, of excessively tight fiscal policy in aggregate, which can exacerbate the debt burden. Because these countries are part of a monetary union there is no easy way for a peripheral group to generate higher nominal GNP growth whilst remaining part of the union. The resulting debt overhang, in light of the widely accepted principle of *lex monatae* (national control of national currency), cannot easily be solved by a simple and terminal exit from the monetary union. Indeed, such an exit would imply an increase in foreign currency debt following any devaluation and in all likelihood result in non-performing assets being held by the nation's creditors. Any such exit would leave any a single country with the twin problems of being small and open and having to build up domestic financial credibility.

Figure 3: The international investment position of various EU states

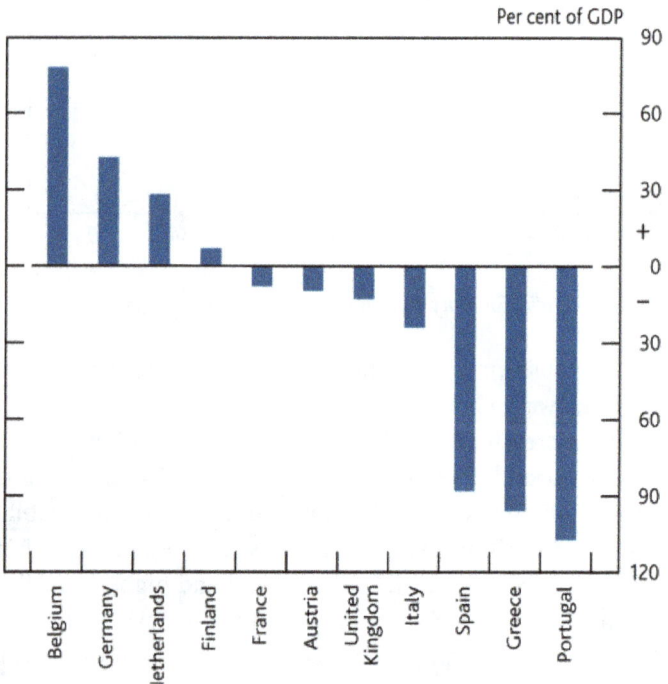

Source: *Financial Stability Review, Bank of England, December 2011*

In this book we shall consider:

(i) The best way to restructure the EMU so that some of the peripheral states can obtain an option to leave on a *temporary* basis;

(ii) How to allow the core Euro states to remain within a monetary union;

(iii) An appropriate way to restructure Euro public and private debt contracts;

(iv) A way to recapitalise banks following a sovereign default or restructuring;

(v) The intermediate requirements for the ultimate creation of a fiscal union;

(vi) The set of policies that should be followed by the ECB; and

(vii) The conditions under which countries would be allowed to rejoin the EMU.

CHAPTER 2
ECONOMIC AND MONETARY UNION:
A PYRRHIC VICTORY

2.1 Problems, problems

The establishment of the EMU was a victory of politics over economics. Stage 3 of Economic and Monetary Union was established in 1999 with 11 nations and a formal opt-out from monetary union for the UK and Denmark.

Figure 4: Surplus and deficit countries in the Eurozone and the world

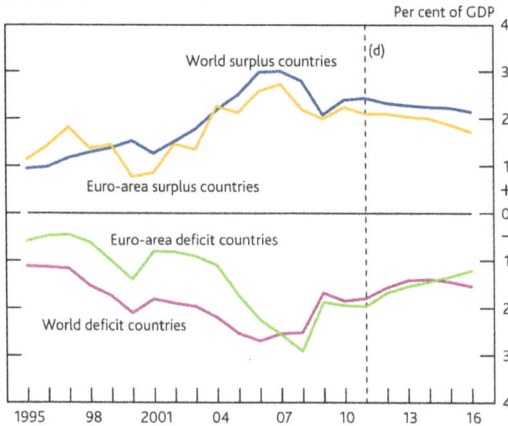

Source: *Financial Stability Review, Bank of England, December 2011*

An extended number of summits to try to solve the crisis in the Eurozone led to the statement by the Euro Heads of State on 9th December 2011, which was an attempt to build a more credible fiscal and stabilisation framework for members, and prospective members, of the Eurozone. However, in many respects this represents a sparse and controversial prescription in advocating fiscal retrenchment with insufficient detail as to how assessment and sanctions are to be performed. The growing sovereign debt crisis in the Eurozone is the result of the build-up of intra-union claims between debtor and creditor nations within the Euro area and the growing perception that public debt levels in many Eurozone economies – exacerbated by ongoing banking problems, as in Ireland and Spain – are nearly, if not absolutely, unsustainable. And so the Eurozone, as a microcosm of the world economy, is split between surplus economies that are growing, or have reasonable prospects of doing so, and deficit economies that are nearly stalling (see Figure 4).

Adjustment would normally involve a lower exchange rate for the deficit nations so that they could share in the potential growth of the surplus nations. Within the Eurozone, intra-union nominal exchange rate adjustment is not possible due to the common currency. Real exchange rate adjustment for deficit nations will require a considerable period of lower inflation than that experienced in surplus nations. With limited price and wage flexibility, such adjustment will require extended periods of lower growth in surplus nations in order to create the required negative output gaps. It is not entirely clear that surplus nations will tolerate the implied reduction in their competitiveness. The duration and severity of the economic downturn associated with the financial crisis of 2007-8 has led to precipitous falls in GDP in many Eurozone economies which had been trying to stabilise their GDP, and thus to strains on already vulnerable fiscal positions. With little or no immediate prospect of growth in nominal GDP, public debt levels in many

Eurozone economies have started to look increasingly unsustainable (see Figure 5).

Figure 5: The change in public indebtedness since the start of the crisis

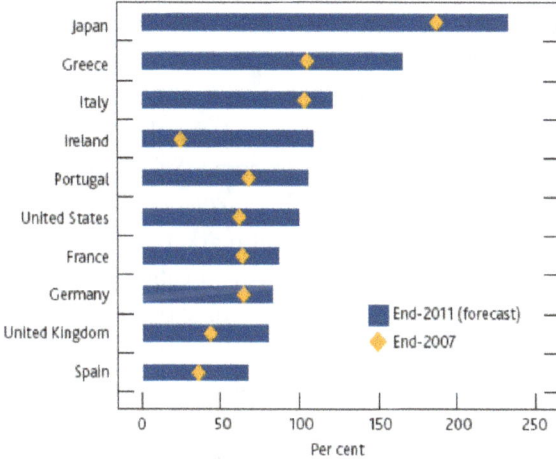

Source: IMF *Fiscal Monitor* (September 2011).

We also wish to stress the addition of a serious banking problem to this real economy payments problem. To say nothing of failing to write off significant quantities of 'toxic' credit derivatives issued and purchased in the build-up to the subprime crisis of 2007-08, highly leveraged European financial institutions are currently holding considerable quantities of national public debt issued by Eurozone member nations. In the early life of the Eurozone, the sovereign debt of member states was eligible collateral in the liquidity operations of the ECB against which no capital provisions had to be made. But as the crisis has deepened, the debt of more peripheral countries has had more restrictions placed on their eligibility by the ECB. This change in the criteria has opened up the ongoing possibility that eligible debt may become ineligible for liquidity operations and reflects the increasingly high possibility of default by a number of Eurozone sovereign nations.

A default on sovereign debt by a Eurozone nation has a number of corollaries. First, the defaulting nation will be unable to access capital markets for some time in order to refinance existing debt or create new debt obligations. Figure 6 shows the extent of sovereign redemptions over the next nine years for the Portugal, Greece, Italy and Spain. With a total of over € 2trn to refinance over this period, the shock of any *one* default will echo for some years to come. Secondly, any one default will heighten the likelihood of *further* defaults and thus may lead to some cessation of capital market access for other Eurozone economies – the incidence of so-called *contagion*. A default will also trigger some calls for capital by banks or other financial institutions that hold the underlying principal. Such calls for capital are then likely to involve claims on the fiscal purse of the country in which the financial institution is regulated and so ultimately underwritten. Note also that payments for any holders of credit default swaps written on the underlying sovereign debt will become due in the event of a default. (We shall return to this point below.)

Figure 6: Sovereign redemptions of peripheral EMU countries over 2012-2020

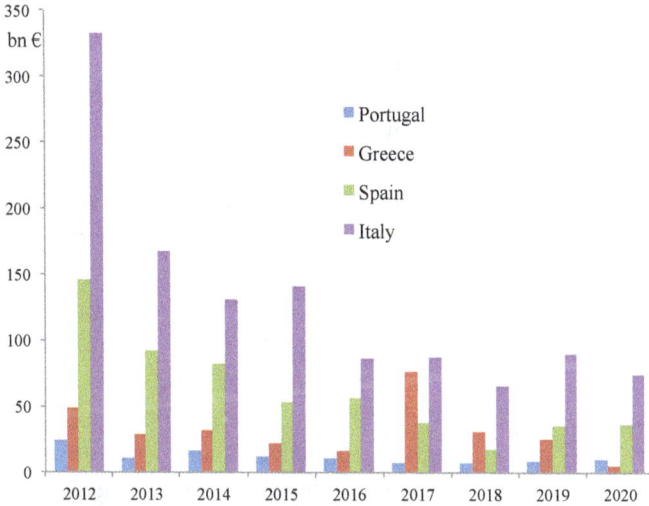

Source: Bloomberg and authors' calculations

The policy response to date has involved the injection of large quantities of liquidity for commercial banks by the ECB, most recently at term, and the creation of stability funds – the EFSF and EFSM, to be succeeded by the European Stability Mechanism (ESM) – to help with the rescue packages for troubled Eurozone economies. The ECB now virtually operates in practice as a lender of last resort for the Eurozone banking system with ongoing development of TARGET2 (Trans-European Automated Real-time Gross settlement Express Transfer) liabilities and the development of the Long Term Refinancing Operations (LTROs). But as Emergency Liquidity Assistance (ELA) remains decentralised to the national central banks and collateral remains with the peripheral national central banks, there are some genuine limits to ECB practice. The recently announced scheme for so-called Outright Monetary Transactions (OMTs) to buy unlimited quantities of government debt at 1- to 3-year maturities from the secondary market as part of a programme of IMF-style conditionality, will help with refinancing operations of severely indebted states by removing from the market debt that would otherwise be approaching redemption. This debt does not then disappear, as it will also require redemption within three years, but such liquidity redemption will allow yet more time for necessary reform.

Note that liquidity provision, per se, cannot be a solution to a structural payments problem within a monetary union, since temporary flows of liquidity cannot clear the stocks of debt. The ECB has also been unable to operate extensive non-conventional monetary policies that involve the purchase of longer-term government bonds in return for reserves, effect swaps of short-term bills for longer-term bonds, or indeed, provide consistent signals about the likely duration of low interest rates in this uncertain economic environment. These policy constraints have exacerbated the problems faced by the more slowly growing or heavily indebted Eurozone economies.

The overall macro-economic and financial picture is thus rather complicated. To sum up:

(i) a significant number of countries in the Eurozone have at present the wrong real exchange rate;

(ii) have been accumulating losses in their net foreign asset position since the inception of EMU;

(iii) are now running up against their sustainable public debt limits relative to their likely nominal GDP growth;

(iv) have significant contingent calls on the public purse from the capital losses likely to be sustained by country-level financial institutions in the event of a default or debt haircut;

(v) are facing increasing problems in financing the primary issuance and the refinancing of public debt and, as a consequence, are paying escalating risk premia; and

(vi) operate within the framework of a central bank that is somewhat hampered with the limited tools and transparency available to its operations.

2.2 Failure of the 2011/12 reforms to date

The Euro Heads of States' statement of 9th December 2011 and the 30th January 2012 Summit is thus deficient in a number of respects. The enhanced successor to the Growth and Stability Pact, which includes both the European Semester and the Euro Plus Pact, together with the new 'fiscal compact', does not really address the problems addressed by the Growth and Stability Pact. It is most important to adopt policies that stabilise the level of public debt *in expectation*, so that forward-looking agents continue to price debt so as to allow sovereign access to capital markets at reasonable spreads. The present situation, spurred by expectations of at least some EMU sovereign default is the exact converse (Di Cesare *et al.*, 2012). However a relatively simple *fiscal* rule for the deficit may not be particularly helpful, as countries display considerable heterogeneity in both initial conditions and likely response to fiscal adjustment.

In fact, a monetary union that does not constitute an optimum currency area will imply *more* rather than less variance in fiscal deficits and surpluses over the business cycle. And although the 'fiscal compact' calls for an upper bound to the structural deficit of 0.5% of nominal GDP, it is in practice very hard to *measure* the deficit in real time. So we may find that the target is not enforceable simply because performance relative to this criterion cannot easily be measured.

In any event, meeting a fiscal deficit target in the form of an upper bound could easily end up being *pro-cyclical*, as the deficit may not get corrected or become a sufficiently large surplus in a boom. How exactly does this fiscal rule enforce sufficient surpluses in the *good times*? If it does not, the rule may well trap economies in a world of permanent deficits. It is of great concern that fiscal rule performance would be judged by the Commission, Council and ultimately, by the Court of Justice. Rather than being an objective in its own right, there is a danger that attesting to its achievement might become one of a number of measures bargained over at the EU level of 17 or 27 nations. We are also concerned as to whether courts or political institutions can move quickly enough to satisfy the worries of market participants. Some form of *Fiscal Council* staffed by economists, some of whom may be drawn from the Commission and national Ministries of Finance, may make considerably more sense.

Simple numerical targets for overall annual deficits of 3% of nominal GDP or debt levels of 60% of nominal GDP are rather attractive long-term targets, as they were for the original Growth and Stability Pact, even though they were virtually immediately violated in several instances, not least by their originating nations. By the same token, the new fiscal compact cannot really be credible unless it deals specifically with the current problem of fiscal consolidation for a large number of Eurozone states and then separately spells out how fiscal deficits and debt levels should be run and monitored within a monetary union in more normal times. If the current `debt overhang' is not addressed, the fiscal compact is unlikely ever to gain credibility.

The development of a permanent successor to the EFSF and EFSM, the ESM, may be helpful and the Summit agreement bringing the permanent support mechanism forward by one year to 2012 is reasonable. But it is a concern that there is limited funding available, currently estimated to be €750bn, not yet in place, and that this size fund may not be sufficiently highly rated by credit agencies to allow it to fund bail-outs or fiscal consolidation across several countries at the same time. In this respect, it is worth recalling that such mechanisms rely too much on the debt quality of stronger countries (through state guarantees), as highlighted by the recent credit downgrading of the EFSF. Such funds ought to address the appropriate construction of bail-outs that help countries finance future fiscal plans that have been formulated with the explicit help and conditionality of the IMF. This will imply helping a country to fund itself after a bail-out and ensuring that the correct monetary-fiscal mix is adopted. There is *no* good economic case – only a *political* one – for the direct purchase of existing sovereign debt from countries with fiscal problems by such funds. As far as it can be seen, the issue of debt restructuring is completely missing in the reports of 9th December 2011 agreement and the 30th January 2012 Summit and, with the exception of the pending Spanish bank recapitalisations, continues to this day.

Table 1: Possible losses from sovereign bond haircuts

Tier 1 capital ratio	7% capital ratio		10% capital ratio	
	50%	50%	50%	50%
Haircut	Greece	PIIGS	Greece	PIIGS
Number of bank failures	45	63	76	80
Capital shortfall (€bn)	-73.86	-278.78	-348.09	-605.68
Total GDP cost	-0.58	-2.19	-2.73	-4.76
of which:				
EMU states (€bn)	-68.45	-270.93	-272.74	-525.53
Non-EMU states (€bn)	-5.31	-7.62	-75.35	-80.16
As % of EU output				
EMU states	-0.54	-2.13	-2.14	-4.13
Non-EMU states	-0.04	-0.06	-0.59	-0.63

Source: Reuters and authors' calculations

Note: PIIGS refers to Portugal, Ireland, Italy, Greece and Spain. The results use market data from the final quarter of 2011 and calculate the resulting losses to banks that hold sovereign debt and the implied cost in terms of Euros and relative to GDP.

It is also rather problematic to have a single ESM for the whole of the Eurozone. Suppose that there is a 50% haircut for Greek debt only. As shown in Table 1, the capital shortfall for the

EU banking system would then be some €74bn at an assumed target core Tier 1 capital ratio of 7%. These losses would rise to nearly €350bn at a target core Tier 1 capital ratio of 10%. If we factored in a much more widespread haircut over time, to include Portugal, Ireland, Italy and Spain as well as Greece, the capital shortfall would be €280bn and over €600bn in the case of a target core Tier 1 capital ratio of 7% and 10% respectively.

However, although the *official* total notional haircut on Greek government debt to date is 53.5%, the actual haircut we calculate to be very nearly 75%, leaving the various bond holders in total with only one quarter of their original notional principal. More precisely, assuming the official remaining principal of €31.5bn, or 46.5% of original notional, was exchanged for new Greek and EFSF bonds on 12 March 2012, the total value of the new bonds is only €25.85bn representing a total net present value (NPV) haircut of 74.15% on total notional principal (see Table 2).

Table 2: Actual NPV haircut on 12.3.12 Greek bond exchange

		New Greek bonds	EFSF 2-year bonds	ESFS 1-year bonds
New principal amount	(€bn)	31.50	7.50	7.50
Valuation discount rate	(%)	12.00	0.90	0.60
New bond price	(% face value)	34.4	100.2	99.8
New bond value	(€bn)	10.85	7.51	7.49
Total value of new bonds: €25.85bn			Total NPV haircut: 74.15%	

Source: Bloomberg and authors' calculations

In general, the ESF fund, as currently envisaged but not yet in place, could very easily be totally exhausted. So it will simply not be credible to financial market participants unless its firepower – i.e. its amount – is increased, with some limited contributions from EU nations that have exercised an opt-out from EMU. Some vague commitment has already been made by the UK, but this is controversial within the coalition government.

The ECB's monetary policy framework has shown insufficient flexibility following the crisis in terms of flexible inflation targeting, using open market operations to influence longer-term interest rates, providing longer-term guidance on the path of short-term interest rates and influencing the Euro exchange rate with respect to the rest of the world. Part of this inflexibility reflects the institutional constraints that are to some extent enshrined in ECB Statutes.

Finally, it seems likely that the whole macro-economic management of the individual nations in the Eurozone is not sufficiently well co-ordinated. For example, it is likely that looser fiscal policy in creditor nations and tighter fiscal policy in debtor nations would have helped adjustment in the debtor nations. Clearly a common monetary policy and national sovereign debt issuance do not sit well together. Nevertheless, it is the case that the increased supply of bonds issued by countries *not* facing debt constraints would have changed the composition of debt issued by Eurozone member states towards the less risky and more liquid, rather than the converse. This would be preferable not only during the crisis but also more generally.

The political debate regarding the consequences of a Greek exit from the Eurozone has moved from total denial of the possibility to assertions that this event could be contained. On the other hand, the IMF reckons that, upon exit, both Greek output and the new drachma would drop precipitously, leading to widespread defaults on foreign currency denominated liabilities. The investment banks Barclays Capital and UBS independently estimate that this in turn would result in an involuntary transfer to Greece from the EU and the ECB of up to €230bn – or about 2.5% of Eurozone GDP. The subsequent course of contagion to other EMU nations is thought by many to be inevitable and to lead to the break-up of the Eurozone with losses to EMU nations of around 12% of total

GDP (*Financial Times*, 18.5.12, p.9). This would represent the failure of the European dream that has evolved over the past 60 years.

Leaving aside the consequences for the 17 nations of the Eurozone, the break-up would imperil half the UK and Chinese exports and a quarter of US exports which go to Europe, to say nothing of the $1.2trn of financial assets in EMU sovereigns and corporations currently held by Americans. Estimates of the impact of a *disorderly* Greek exit from the Eurozone range from 5 to 10 times that of the events in September 2008 surrounding the Lehmans collapse, to a *total* freeze-up and collapse of global financial markets. In our opinion, an unmanaged summary exit of Greece from the Eurozone would be an unmitigated global disaster.

We therefore propose the creation of a reset option applicable to *all* members of EMU. This would mean that the current monetary union would rapidly, but transparently, evolve to one comprising a 'hard' currency union that will retain the Euro as the means of payment, unit of account and medium of exchange, and a 'soft' currency zone in which individual sovereign currencies will be reissued and pegged to the Euro in a muddy float under IMF surveillance and the supervision of two new EU institutions, a Fiscal Council and a Sovereign Bankruptcy Court. The 'hard' currency union will still operate largely as the current wider EMU, but this will require explicit adoption of lender of last resort functions for the ECB, banking system consolidation and adoption of more transparent and forward-looking monetary policy-making, clear fiscal rules on debt levels and a central counterparty for monetary operations for the national central banks in the currency zone. Future membership of the hard currency union will remain an *aspiration* for members of the soft currency zone and it is expected that over time they will migrate back to EMU at an appropriate exchange rate to be determined at rejoining. In effect, we favour the creation of a Stage 3a and 3b for EMU, corresponding to the hard and soft currency zones respectively, for which Treaty Reform will be required; Denmark and the UK will retain their opt-outs.

EMU member countries with significant payment problems would then have a third option to add to the current configuration. The current two options are to stay in the current EMU set-up without the ability to correct a significant appreciation or payments problem, or alternatively to leave once and for all the EMU and the EU and face severe credibility problems in the development of monetary and fiscal policies (*Financial Times*, 18.5.12, p.9). The new reset option will involve leaving the 'hard currency zone' *temporarily*. The leaver will adopt an agreed haircut on the principal of their Euro-denominated debt and the resulting debts will be transferred into new Euro-denominated bonds of various maturities with their principals jointly and severally guaranteed by the 'hard currency' EMU nations (as has been approximately attempted by Greece). A debt advisory committee of the new European Bankruptcy Court, in conjunction with the new Fiscal Council and the IMF, will advise on the scale of the haircut and also on the appropriate issuance of bonds. The countries that choose to enter this holding pen will issue their own domestic currency, but it will be pegged to the Euro with the exchange rate bands set with the advice of the new institutions. The country will have access to IMF funding and be subject to rigorous surveillance on both monetary issuance and fiscal plans. Some form of capital controls will be required for countries using the reset option, which will involve higher capital and liquidity requirements.

Conditions for re-entry to the hard Euro zone will include stricter conditions for entry in terms of economic convergence, with subsequent enhanced fiscal surveillance from the Fiscal Council. Although a country may have the aim of returning to EMU at the exchange rate which was originally fixed, in many cases this unrealistic original exchange rate will likely require significant adjustment for re-entry. Our solution will maintain the overall momentum of EMU, but will also allow some breathing space for stressed countries to reconfigure their economic institutions.

Any solution to the EMU problem must adopt a two-stage reform. First, there needs to be a wholesale examination of the current monetary and fiscal settlements in the EMU, which we term *institution building*, and then, with agreement upon the form of the new and revised institutions, the parallel development of a reset option for poorly performing economies. In all cases, the levels of sovereign debt will have escalated for nearly all economies and some form of extended fiscal consolidation will be required, even for those economies that do not utilise the reset option.

CHAPTER 3
INSTITUTION BUILDING

3.1 European Central Bank reforms

As NOTED ABOVE, the ECB is already effectively acting as
the lender of last resort to the EMU financial system (and
beyond) in the traditional sense. This should be made *explicit*
by appropriate changes to the ECB Constitution through EMU
negotiation and agreement as soon as possible. In our opinion
the ECB should *never* lend to EMU governments by buying
their bonds *directly* – this is a step in the wrong direction for a
fully functioning central bank! Direct governmental purchase
of sovereign debt is a matter for other EMU mechanisms
begun – but by no means completed – at Lisbon. Currently
the measures proposed for the European Stability Facility are
the effective merging of EFSF and ESM funds with a total capital of about €750bn – at 8% of current €9.2trn EMU GDP not
nearly enough – to make loans to sovereigns against government bond collateral and to undertake other fiscal measures.

On the other hand, we believe that EMU nations should
agree as soon as possible to amend the Constitution of the ECB
to modify the TARGET2 payments system structure so that
transfers do not simply *pass through* the ECB. This would eliminate bilateral national central bank deficits and surpluses such

as those currently between Ireland and Greece with Germany (Scott, 1998).

In more detail, the TARGET2 system is the gross inter-bank clearing settlement system which, after its introduction in November 2007, has been used by all the national central banks (NCBs) in the Euro system, except Sweden and the UK, since May 2008. The ECB requires that the TARGET system be used for all payments between Euro system institutions. The Bundesbank, Banque de France and Banc d'Italia built, own and run the system for, and on behalf of, the European System of Central Banks (ESCB), which includes all central banks in the EU. It is used by both NCBs and individual banks to clear and settle Euro transactions between each other. Each NCB in the Euro system, as well as the ECB itself, operates a national component system. Under the terms of a Euro system agreement, the outstanding claims and liabilities of all the national central banks participating in TARGET2 are transferred to the ECB at the end of a business day and netted out.

NCBs are responsible for providing liquidity to their national banking systems. When an Irish bank repos securities it does so with the Central Bank of Ireland (CBI). The liquidity that the CBI generates for the bank doesn't necessarily remain in the Irish banking system; for example, it might be used to pay an import bill from Germany, buy a fund in Luxembourg, or be moved to create a deposit in the Netherlands. Having automatic balances within the TARGET system means that NCBs automatically have access to *all* the funds they need.

If the CBI had to settle all its TARGET2 balances then it would have to borrow the funds. The ECB could in theory lend the CBI the money (in which case the system would be similar to the US Federal Reserve System) or it would have to negotiate borrowing the money from other NCBs with surpluses. The latter solution would be impractical, and would risk settlement failure if the required funds could not be obtained. The former arrangement would mean that the ECB would have a much bigger balance sheet, but it is consistent with the role of the central bank of a currency union.

The original TARGET system was built by linking together the different real time gross system (RTGS) structures that existed at the national level and meant that the NCBs would have gross claims against each other through correspondent accounts. TARGET2 has evolved so that claims are netted off against each other daily and become claims and liabilities to the system itself.

Market economists often refer to the "ECB's balance sheet". In practice they are usually referring to the *consolidated* balance sheet of the Euro system. The consolidated balance sheet will by definition not have any TARGET2 balances since the surpluses of some NCBs will be perfectly offset by the deficits of other NCBs.[1] The consolidated balance sheet of the ECB therefore fails to show the growing complexity and dynamics underlying the Euro system's balance sheet. As Sinn and Wollmershauser (2011) point out, TARGET2 balances will reflect the *accumulated* deficits and surpluses in each EMU country's balance of payments with the rest of the Eurozone (see Figure 8). Following the financial crisis of 2007-2008, the ability of financial markets to recirculate current account balances via inter-bank lending and portfolio investment has been seriously weakened. Moreover, money market lending to banks by both the US and within the EU used for these purposes has been halved from pre-crisis levels.

The corollary of a current account *deficit* is that investment in that country is greater than its savings. If the additional investment is financed by bank loans which are then repo-ed with its central bank, then the central bank will find that liquidity has left the banking system and it will have a short-age of funds which it must then obtain through TARGET2. At the same time as private capital market intermediation broke

---

1   Non-EMU Target2 members will have small balances within the TARGET system.

down, the ECB introduced a range of alternative policy tools, such as long-term repos, which increased the ability of NCBs to finance their domestic financial systems. This in turn has led to a large increase in the size of the consolidated balance sheet of the Euro system.

Figure 7: Consolidated financial statement of the Euro system: breakdown of assets

Source: Bloomberg and authors' calculations

This growth in the Euro system's balance sheet has had important implications for TARGET2 balances (see Figure 8). The 'other assets' item of the Euro system balance sheet, which is essentially the balance the Bundesbank has with the TARGET2 system, reached €494.3bn at the end of December 2011.[2] Since then, the ECB had its first 3-year LTRO of €489bn. When the

---

2   Other assets include claims due to the difference between monetary income to be pooled and redistributed. This is only relevant for the period between booking of monetary income as part of the year-end procedures, and its settlement on the last working day in January each year. Other intra-Euro system claims denominated in Euros may arise, including the interim distribution of ECB income.

sum of the ECB's main and long-term refinancing operations jumped by a net €75bn in September 2011, the Bundesbank's TARGET2 balance increased by €60bn. An exact ratio between these two levels is unlikely to hold, since following a repo by a non-German bank, it will not necessarily wish to use all the funds immediately, and cash balances with its NCB will grow temporarily. However, as these funds are drawn down by the bank, ECB deposits will fall, increasing the national central bank's liabilities with the Bundesbank. If this has taken place for the second round of LTRO in February, it could imply at least a further €390bn increase has taken place in the Bundesbank's positive balance in TARGET2, perhaps taking it to well over €800bn.

Figure 8: Cumulated EMU national TARGET2 balances

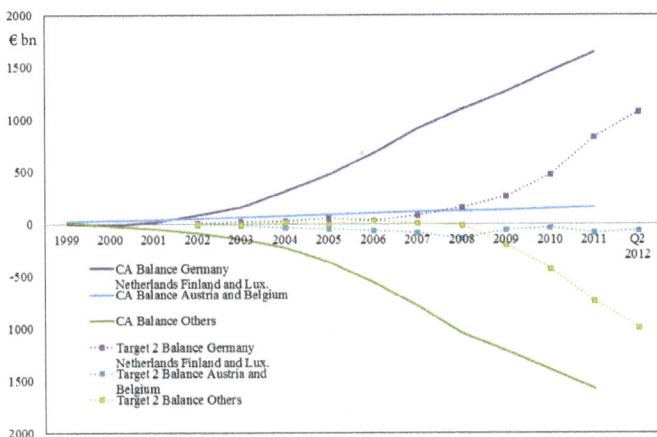

Source: Bloomberg and authors' calculations

This second LTRO tranche was €530bn for a total of about €1trn, which is not much greater than half the $2trn the Federal Reserve pumped into the US financial system in 2008-9, some of which at the time was of course used by European banks.

On the other hand, what happens if a national central bank goes bankrupt, or if the Euro ceases to exist, is not well specified in the Maastricht treaty. This lending is not collateralised and so is far from riskless. Article 32 of the Constitution of the ECB allows for losses to be shared by NCBs:

> "The Governing Council may decide that national central banks shall be indemnified against costs incurred in connection with the issue of banknotes or, in exceptional circumstances, for specific losses arising from monetary policy operations undertaken for the ESCB (Euro system). Indemnification shall be in a form deemed appropriate in the judgment of the Governing Council; but these amounts may be offset against the national central banks' monetary income."

The Bundesbank therefore currently argues that an actual loss will be incurred only if and when a Euro system counterparty defaults and the collateral it has posted, despite the risk control measures applied by the system, does not realise the full value of the collateralised refinancing operations. Any actual loss would however always be borne by the Euro system as a *whole*, regardless of which national bank records it. The cost of such a loss would be shared among the national banks in line with their capital keys. In other words, the Bundesbank's risk position of 13% of notional would be just the same if the positive settlement balance from TARGET2 were accrued, not by the Bundesbank, but instead by another Euro system national bank. However, in a situation where the Euro system ceases to exist, it is not clear how the guarantees would be enforced. These considerations are highly relevant to the recent repatriations of capital from Greece and Spain by French and German banks.

The IFO (Sinn and Wollmershaeuser, 2011) assert that the Bundesbank's credit in TARGET2 is causing a credit crunch in

Germany and that Germany is essentially funding the deficits of other Euro zone countries for free. They argue that:

> "Aggregated over the period 2008-2010, the current account deficits of Greece and Portugal were financed practically in their entirety by the printing press... from 2008-2010 Germany accumulated a current account surplus of 264 billion euros vis-a-vis other Eurozone countries, but in net terms this did not translate into it acquiring titles abroad, such as factories, real estate or securities. Instead fully 255 billion euros...was "settled" with Target claims of the Bundesbank on the ECB."

However, by concentrating on the *net* figures the IFO ignores some other important flows. Since the end of Q4 2007, German Federal bonds and notes have increased by over €340bn. With German Treasury bills having negative yields and the 2-year note now at 13.4 basis points, the German public sector, including the Bundesbank, is no worse on a *flow* basis. At a time when there has been significant balance sheet contraction in international banking, German Monetary Financial Institutions (MFIs, essentially banks) have seen an increase in their liabilities. We believe that this has been driven by 'safe haven' demand from investors, and hence has been on beneficial terms for German banks. Of course, if the Bundesbank was to make capital losses on these exposures, then these would be far greater than the differences in rates on the flows.

Losses on TARGET2 balances could be substantial. Econometric evidence suggests that cumulative current account balances show not only a good relationship with TARGET2 balances but also with 10-year benchmark spreads over the Bund. If we look at the National Bank of Greece's balance sheet, for example, we see that its main assets are 'deposits' and lending to Greek banks. If Greece were to leave the Euro, these assets would likely be redenominated and Greek Government bonds would have to be written down significantly. Only 13%

of the Bank of Greece's assets are foreign or gold. A Greek exit from the EMU would likely require exit from TARGET2, forcing a write-down on Euro system exposures to Greece, as noted above. Losses in excess of the ECB's capital and reserves were never really envisaged and the mechanisms to transfer losses are not well specified. An exact estimate of the losses is dependent on lots of unknowables: the size of TARGET2 balances at the point of break-up, the number of countries leaving the EMU, the size of depreciations following their exit, and the financial position of the NCBs, which will in turn be dependent on haircuts on sovereign and financial exposure. Each such leaver will require stop-gap measures which will significantly impact the balance sheet of the ECB.

We therefore believe for the future that an important reform to the modification of the articles governing the ECB is a modification of the TARGET2 structure so that each national central bank in the system would trade *directly* with the ECB through a pooled ECB account, thereby eliminating bilateral central bank deficits and surpluses, such as those currently between Ireland and Greece with Germany, and allowing the ECB to monitor the decline of individual sovereign creditworthiness directly (Scott, 1998). The concomitant expansion of the ECB's balance sheet is consistent with its functioning as the central bank of a currency union along the lines of the UK Bank of England and the US Federal Reserve. However, some form of quarterly settlement of TARGET2 balances, such as takes place between US Federal Reserve banks, will be necessary to maintain the market's credibility regarding the Euro system and to limit the ECB's balance sheet expansion.

3.2 European financial system regulation

The Eurozone sovereign debt crisis has exposed many problems with the previous regulatory regime and the new one currently being constructed. Whilst it is quite right that financial intermediaries build up capital and liquidity to deal with excessive levels of leverage and to meet deposit calls, the abundant supply of sovereign debt does not meet both these needs. Specifically, sovereign debt can no longer be considered risk-free in all states of nature and so cannot be used to source liquidity. And in fact, the concurrent economic and sovereign debt crisis has mean that government debt has tended to become more risky and illiquid exactly when it is most required to perform that role. In this sense, the role of government debt must be fundamentally reconsidered. This has implications for both reform and reset.

So before setting out our recommendations on financial derivatives based on sovereign debt and governmental institutions, we briefly consider here pending global and EU regulations regarding banking, insurance, financial instruments and trading. Perhaps the most important of these are the developing international ramifications of the US Dodd-Frank Act and the Basel III recommendations of the Bank of International Settlements, although in Europe there is a smorgasbord of developing (sometimes in our opinion inconsistent or mistaken) regulation with acronyms like, for example, Solvency II, MiFID2, Tobin (Transactions) Tax, MiFIR, Prips, etc.[3] How a 'banking union' within Europe would work under the reset framework is also crucially important. A full survey is beyond the scope of this book but we do wish to highlight a couple of ways in which the correct specification of financial market regulation will be crucial to the satisfactory working of reset.

---

3   MiFID2 is the Markets in Financial Instruments Directive 2, is due to be implemented late this year and updates MiFID which was implemented in 2007. MiFIR is Markets in Financial Instruments Regulation and will be implemented alongside MiFID2. Packaged Retail Investment Products (Prips) are the subject of European legislation by the Commission to ensure similar treatment for investor protection and standards of disclosure for structured financial products.

The Basel III proposals consist of five main pillars:

I. Raising the quality and quantity of capital;

II. Improving credit risk management, including the creation of the credit valuation adjustment (CVA) whereby capital for counterparty risk is adjusted according to changes in the market perception of the credit worthiness of that counterparty;

III. Limits on over-all leverage through;

IV. Macro-prudential measures including counter-cyclical capital requirements;

V. Improvements in liquidity management through the liquidity coverage ratio (LCR: the requirement for banks to hold high quality liquid assets in a sufficient quantity to meet anticipated cash outflows, including lines of credit and other undrawn commitments over a 30-day stress period) and the net stable funding ratio (NSFR: the requirement for banks to hold equity, customer deposits and long-term wholesale funding above 100% of their long-term assets).

The first lesson for bank regulation from the Eurozone crisis is that AAA to AA rated sovereign securities do *not* have the zero credit risk implicit in their zero risk weighting in Basel II risk weighted asset calculations. Spanish Government bonds were AAA rated as recently as January 2009. In Europe the mistake was compounded by the EU's Capital Requirement's Directive (CRD), which wrongly gave all Eurozone sovereign exposure a zero weight, so even Greece, which had a rating at best of A from S&P back in 2001, still carried a zero weighting. The Eurozone sovereign debt crisis reminds us that investing in states can be risky, with default or haircuts distinctly possible, and so capital provision for holding them needs to be made.

Our reset and reform proposals make the credit risk in sovereigns more explicit. The draft proposals in the most recent CRD IV are possibly too tough in certain respects. In particular, the use of CDS spreads in the calculation of 'credit valuation adjustments', the amount of additional capital to be held when a credit exposure deteriorates, opens up the use of illiquid CDS prices being manipulated to induce 'bear raids' (a problem with CDS pricing that we will discuss in the next section). However, the CRD currently exempts sovereign exposures leading to inadequate capital to require capital being held against these risks. The 'large exposures regime' (LER) limits any individual exposure representing more than 25% of equity and also exempts sovereign exposure. This means that the CRD, the large exposures regime and Basel III in general are inappropriate for our new reset proposals and would need to be strengthened further. In particular we suggest that sovereign exposure to an entity which is rated below AA- is subject to a relatively low maximum, say 25% of equity, and a single sovereign exposure of a rating AA- or better is capped at 100% of equity. This would require significant modification to the LCR, since sovereign assets are the main instrument used to achieve a sufficient level of liquid capital to meet this objective. We therefore propose that the LCR allows a broader range of assets which can meet liquidity requirements, but, given the greater volatility in the value of these assets, that appropriate haircuts will have to be applied.

Our reset proposals also make implicit risks more *explicit*, because government debt can be forgiven and lose its underlying capital value. Whilst we do not believe that these proposals raise overall risk, they do expose the fact that overall equity within the banking system is inadequate. Total equity ratios probably need to be in double digits in order to control for these exposures. We also need to reconcile our reset with the proposals on a banking union with EU-wide deposit insurance. Reset would raise the cost of insuring deposits as there is an explicit redomination risk. Yet without this insurance, banking systems would become more vulnerable to runs. Our historical survey shows that expectations of currency union break-ups (see Section 4.4) can involve substantial capital movements, both in anticipation of a break-up and whilst currency is being redenominated.

An important advantage of the reset mechanism is that under it, the size of the currency depreciation is likely to be much smaller than that of an uncontrolled exit with no expectation of ever returning to EMU and an immediate fear of seignoriage being used to finance deficits. On the other hand, agents will know that their deposits might be redenominated and so will have an incentive to hold them in EMU core institutions rather than in peripheral member state banks. Given the continued growth in TARGET2 balances, an exit is likely to impose substantial costs on the Euro system in any event. A degree of risk sharing for redenomination risk on deposits could therefore be optimal.

A possible compromise might operate along the following lines. Deposits which had a maturity of over one year, and all fixed income assets, become redenominated without compensation. Deposits which had less than one year maturity when taken out will be entitled to compensation based on the change in the value of the currency from the redenomination rate and the average exchange rate on the day that the new currency first trades. One third of the loss will be covered by the banks themselves, one third by the deposit insurance scheme, up to a maximum of €200,000 per individual, with the remaining risk borne by depositors. Since deposits over one year will be riskier for depositors, we suspect that these will be more costly for banks. In order to incentivise banks not to overly fund in shorter-term deposits, only deposits over a year will fully count towards the net stable funding ratio (NSFR) but with a proportion of the shorter-term deposits covered. In attempting to achieve this tougher NSFR the fear will be that banks will achieve this requirement not through raising more equity and seeking longer-term deposits and borrowing, but rather through cutting the asset side of their balance sheet, i.e. lending. This would add to deflationary pressures within the periphery. In order to make quick progress, we suggest that a minimum of any shortfall need be corrected through equity issuance by the time reset is implemented.

Regarding the ongoing important, necessarily complex, implementation of Central Clearing Parties (CCPs) required for derivatives which are currently traded over-the-counter (OTC) by Dodd-Frank, we can see both pros and cons in the concept. On the one hand, this should increase the transparency of trading in complex products, with the concomitants of reduced oligopolistic dealer profits and an increase in the widespread legitimate use of derivative products for hedging financial positions. On the other, the proliferation of multiple derivative trading platforms can lead to confusion and unintended consequences, such as the development of dark pools and the 2010 flash crash in equity trading, to say nothing of the greatly increased systemic default risk of trading platforms and their clearers who will require substantial capital. In any event, the actual extent of the domain of CCPs in terms of derivative product types is highly controversial and already subject to several reversals of position by the US Commodity Futures Trading Commission (CFTC) which has responsibility for implementing the Dodd-Frank derivative recommendations.

3.3 European derivative legislation

A current area of European contention is the extent to which OTC derivative transactions, in particular sovereign Credit Default Swaps (CDS), have exacerbated stress in Eurozone sovereign debt markets.

A *swap* involves the exchange of two sets of cash flows usually with equivalent NPVs. Most often the two cash flows represent a fixed and a floating interest rate on the same *notional* principal (currently about $420trn total notional in interest rate swaps globally – nearly seven times global GDP). In the case of a CDS, the buyer of the CDS makes a series of payments to the writer of a CDS in return for compensation upon the occurrence of a credit event in the underlying reference entity. This compensation usually takes the form of the ability to sell a debt security issued by the entity to the issuer at the notional value of the bond. Figure 9 is a schema illustrating a typical CDS structure.

Figure 9: Structure of a credit default swap

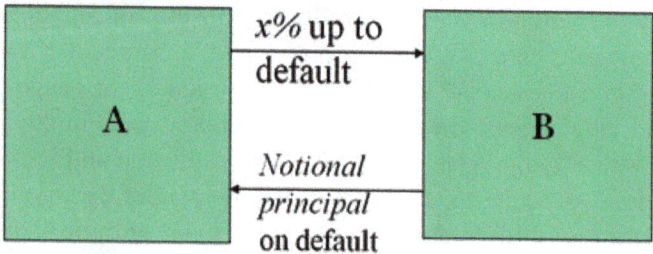

Party A, the protection *buyer*, pays Party B, the protection *seller*, x % per annum up to a *default event*, i.e. a failure by the issuer to honour the underlying bond's obligations. To holders of the underlying sovereign bond, CDS contracts can be used to hedge the credit risk of sovereign default events, as what is lost from the face value of the defaulted bond will be covered by Party B's payment of a the notional principal minus the value of the bond defaulted upon in the default event. As a sovereign's credit deteriorates, the price of this protection rises. This raises the NPV of the purchaser in the CDS contract. Typically, the seller will then post collateral with the purchaser of the protection. Similarly, a fall in the cost of protection will reduce the NPV of the contract and the purchaser will post collateral with the seller. CDS markets create an instrument not only to insure against credit default, but also to facilitate speculation on how the cost of insuring sovereign debt is likely to evolve. To the extent that there can be multiple equilbria in markets, this speculation may not be desirable (see Figures 10 and 11).

These figures show respectively that 5-year and 3-year CDS spreads of the PIIGS nations' sovereign bonds over the CDS rate of German bunds over the crisis period. Until the Lehman default these spreads were negligible, but subsequently the divergence of these default 'insurance' premia at both maturities have broadly mirrored the underlying sovereign bond rates (see Figure 1) and each other. Of course, the International Swaps and Derivatives Association (ISDA), eventually, defined Greece as in default at its sovereign bond restructuring in March 2012 (see Table 2) which triggered Greek CDS payments to remove these instruments from the market, at least until further developments.

Figure 10: 5-year CDS PIIGS spreads

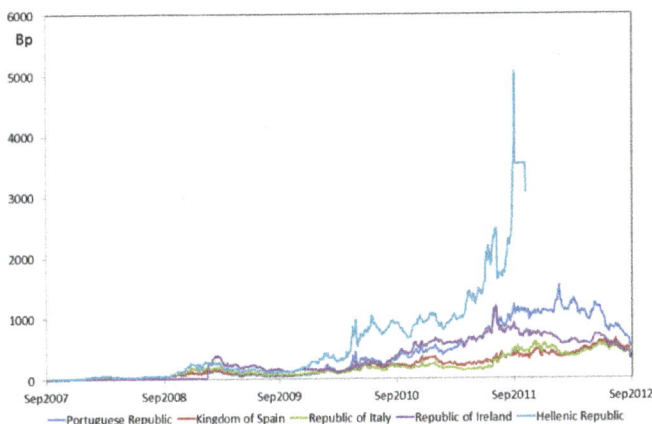

Source: Bloomberg and authors' calculations

Figure 11: 3-year CDS PIIGS spreads

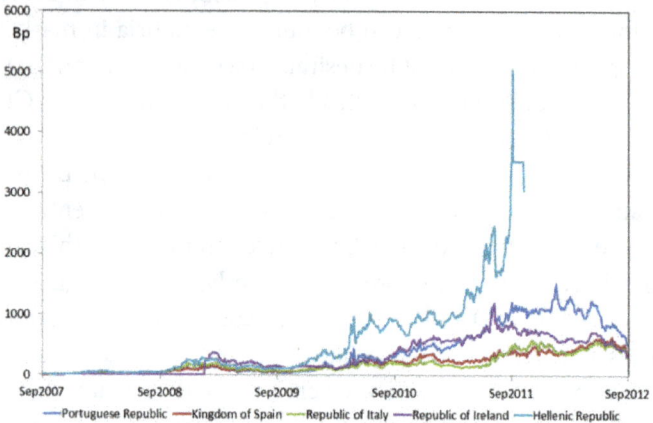

Source: Bloomberg and authors' calculations

The EU has introduced short selling restrictions (Regulation No 236/2012) in an attempt to stop sovereign CDS being used as a speculative instrument:

> "Buying credit default swaps without having a long position in underlying sovereign debt (n) or any assets, portfolio of assets, financial obligations or financial contracts the value of which is correlated to the value of the sovereign debt, can be, economically speaking, equivalent to taking a short position on the underlying debt instrument."

It goes on to argue:

> "Uncovered short selling of shares and sovereign debt is sometimes viewed as increasing the potential risk of settlement failure and volatility. To reduce such risks it is appropriate to place proportionate restrictions on uncovered short selling of such instruments"

and:

"Since entering into a sovereign credit default swap without underlying exposure to the risk of a decline in the value of the sovereign debt could have an adverse impact on the stability of sovereign debt markets, natural or legal persons should be prohibited from entering into such uncovered credit default swap positions."

By separating funding and 'risk-free' interest rate risk from credit risk, CDS should enable sovereign credit risk to sit with those investors who most wish to bear it, and therefore reduce risk premia and lower the cost of government funding. Given heterogeneous views about the relative likelihoods of different economic scenarios and their impact on asset markets, it would at first sight make sense to enable both long and short positions through the CDS market.

However, a number of commentators have pointed out that the CDS markets may have had a destabilising impact on both the 2008 financial crisis and the Eurozone sovereign crisis. Self-fulfilling bear raids can occur in which speculators take an aggressive negative view on a credit, thereby forcing the price of insurance up. By triggering stop-losses (a strategy where writers of protection automatically buy back their protection if a certain level is hit), the speculator is able to close out the position at a profit. Worse still, CDS markets often lack liquidity and very small positions can end up having a disproportionate impact on price, which then impacts related security prices. For example, a short-seller of a more liquid instrument such as Spanish bank equities can create a sell-off in that security by selling illiquid CDS on Spanish bank debt, resulting in a surge in the price of insurance on that name and creating concerns about the creditworthiness of that entity. Although such behaviour is prohibited by market abuse regulations, in practice it may be very difficult for regulators to identify and stop. The potential for CDS to be misused suggests that banning 'uncovered' or 'naked' sovereign CDS purchases might help markets converge on a more stable equilibrium.

However, we wonder if the focus on the problems uncovered by sovereign CDS distracts from even more serious problems with the functioning of the debt markets. Part of the Eurozone's problems came from an over-compression in sovereign spreads over the period of 1998 to mid-2008 (see Figure 1). Sovereign bond markets failed to discipline governments by pricing with higher rates those governments with unsustainable fiscal policies. Higher rates would have led in turn to greater debt servicing costs, which would either have forced smaller primary deficits or fed back into higher deficits. This would have meant that either corrective action or restructuring would have occurred at far lower debt levels and hence lessened the systemic implications of a blow-up.

Failures in the regulatory regime on derivatives have other macro impacts. By varying the parameters of the structures the issuers can skew the mark-to-market (MTM) values and relative risks, both initially and over time. The practice of using OTC swaps with off-market interest rates or exchange rates without explicit recognition of the *fees* involved as a form of debt, so-called 'Tobashi swaps', has become relatively widespread at all levels of government in the EU. A Tobashi swap (Japanese for 'fly away'), as first used in the 1990s by Japanese corporations to hide debt after the property bubble burst, involves one or both sets of cash flows off-market with the NPV of the two flows not the same. The difference in favour of the issuer represents the initial MTM value of the deal and is paid in cash by the dealer (e.g. by Goldman Sachs to Greece and Italy) to the counterparty as an upfront 'fee' for this amount. Since in their swap payments the counterparty will eventually repay this 'fee' over time, it is really a *loan*. However, it is often not recognised as such and has been used, with the aid of leading investment banks, by a number of EMU nations to fudge sovereign debt figures at critical times. In 2010 Eurostat gained the right to audit EU countries' financial data.

> "In the largest derivative transaction disclosed so far, Greece borrowed 2.8 billion euros from Goldman Sachs Inc. group in 2001 [after Papandreou's Pasok party was elected in October 2009] through a derivative that swapped dollar- and yen-denominated debt issued by the nation for euros using a historical exchange rate, a move that generated an implied reduction in total borrowings." (Bloomberg News, 14.6.12)

Of course genuine, often exorbitant, issuer fees are contained in such transactions at taxpayers' expense. In the interests of future transparency, these swaps should be banned by the EU.

As well as hiding the size of government debts using Tobashi swaps, the apparent cost of sovereign borrowing can be disguised by 'cheapening up' a structure through selling CDS, or interest rate caps or floors. The asymmetry of information between the issuing bank and a non-bank client about the respective future risks and obligations of the counterparties is often enormous, not least because of the designed complexity of the contracts. The true cost and risks of Tobashi-type structures may not be apparent to the governments that undertake them, nor indeed to the broader markets from which they are attempting to hide the size or cost of debt. This has led recently to a series of costly closings-out of derivative positions:

- The Italian government, the second most indebted nation in the EU with a current debt of about $2.5trn, paid Morgan Stanley $3.4bn – half its projected annual revenue from its recent austerity VAT increase – to close out OTC swap positions on which Bloomberg News estimates Italy to have previously lost $31bn at current market values (see Bloomberg News, 16.3.12).

- The City of Milan recently sold JP Morgan Chase and Deutsche Bank CDS protection on Italian government bonds (see Bloomberg News, 12.4.12).

- Sicily, Italy's poorest region, has recently obtained €400m from the central government, in part to offset rapidly mounting losses on $1.1bn notional derivative contracts with six banks, led by Bank of America Merrill Lynch, Deutsche Bank and Nomura, based on underlying loans of €2.5bn from state-owned lender Cassa Depositi e Prestiti. Sicily has borrowed a further € 2.5bn from Rome, €147m from Dexia, €347m from the European Investment Bank and has €225m in outstanding bonds. Italy's Prime Minister, Mario Monti, has warned that, with the recent rapid increase of Sicily's €5.3bn debt, he had "serious concerns about the possibility that Sicily could default". Sicily is seeking recourse through criminal court action against the banks (see Bloomberg News, 19.7.12).

Figure 12 shows global credit default swap positions for EMU nations as of 20th January 2012 – expressed in both total outstanding notional and net positions. While some of these net positions are substantial, e.g. for France, Germany and the UK, as well as for Italy and Spain, that of Greece, while nontrivial, is *not*.

Figure12: Global outstanding notional and net CDS positions
on European sovereign debt

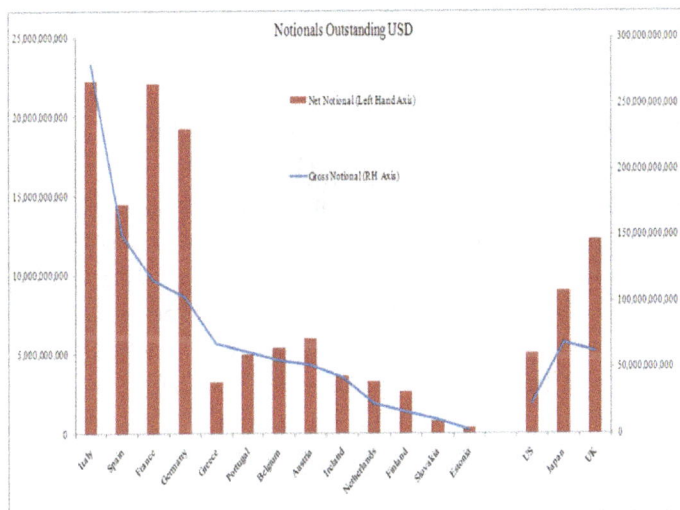

Source: DTCC and authors' calculations

US banks are only minimally directly exposed to European government debt, but they have been buying and selling default protection on these bonds in the form of off-balance sheet CDS. Therefore, while figures are hard to obtain, it has more recently been estimated that for six bulge bracket US institutions, gross CDS exposure on Italian debt alone may be about $200bn (*cf.* Figure 12) and that all US banks account for about two-thirds of the net total of $144bn CDS outstanding on Euro debt (Wallace, 2012). Many troubled European banks have sold significant amounts of CDS protection on their *own* national government's debt – a troubling fact. For example, BNP Paribas has sold $4bn protection on French government debt (12% of the total outstanding) and Banca Monte dei Paschi di Sienna has sold $3bn in Italian government debt (14% of the total outstanding). It has been observed that selling these CDS deals is lucrative and that if either government defaults, the corresponding national banking system will collapse in any event.

We believe *in principle* that banks being *net* sellers of sovereign CDS is likely to increase systemic risk within the financial system. Funding costs for banks are usually positively correlated to the costs of their host country's funding. Banning banks from being net writers of CDS in the sovereign name of the country where they are either domiciled, or have extensive operations, would reduce the probability of making large trading losses at the same time as the cost of their funding increases. Given that in times of stress CDS prices are likely to be positively correlated it would seem expedient also to ban banks from being net sellers of sovereign CDS *overall*. This would require banks to either be prevented from net selling CDS in *any* sovereign name or to enable them to hold only 'naked' long CDS positions in some names to offset CDS that are written on other names. The former requirement would reduce liquidity in CDS markets still further and make manipulation of these markets by entities operating outside European regulatory control still easier. The latter policy would conflict with the rules against naked CDS purchasing cited above.

However, we believe that a tightening-up of rules on market abuse is the best way to tackle such behaviour in lieu of rules which could have unintended consequences. Greater disclosure of all positioning would highlight instances where a market may be being manipulated. Banning a naked CDS position when a short position is held in a correlated security would prevent the manipulation of the CDS market to create price action elsewhere.

Self-fulfilling bear raids could be made more difficult by requiring that all naked long CDS positions must be held for a minimum of three months. This would reduce the ability of speculators to force prices through stop-losses in order to take a quick profit. A period of three months would enable other market participants to identify and research discrepancies and take the other side if the CDS price did not reflect fundamentals.

Other EU regulation of OTC structured derivative selling is also likely to be necessary to enhance investor protection by decreasing information asymmetry through better product description and transparency (Dempster *et al.*, 2011). The principle behind all these recommendations taken together (which make more sense to us than the proposed Tobin tax on all EU financial transactions) is that the role of sovereigns, albeit under economic pressure to consolidate over time like corporations, are not corporations, in that they have a duty to *all* their citizens in *perpetuity* (Graeber, 2011). Government debts are therefore not a legitimate object of global speculation, but knee-jerk regulations restricting the proper functioning of financial markets will ultimately prove to be to the detriment of global welfare.

3.4 European Sovereign Fiscal Council establishment

In the next section of this book we shall outline our recommendations for handling the current Greek and other difficulties to the benefit of the EMU population. Here we stress that we are recommending a new fiscal oversight institution whose role regarding all EMU nations, large and small, we see as critical to a future for EMU.

First, we note that it is now widely accepted that virtually all EMU nations, including France and Germany, breached the 3% of GDP government deficit rule soon after the Maastricht treaty was signed. Further, in this regard much creative accounting has been employed to date by most nations, most notably by Greece, aided by Wall Street at EMU entry in 2001 and subsequently, as the most extreme case. This does not bode well for the proposed 0.5% deficit rule of the new EMU agreement (although we observe that the strictly enforced balanced-budget rules of US states have functioned reasonably well until the recent crisis, which they have exacerbated).

The current EMU situation therefore cries out for an *independent* stand-alone European Sovereign Fiscal Council, along the lines of the new UK counterpart Office for Budget Responsibility (OBR). The new Fiscal Council would be staffed by appropriately competent professional staff drawn from the EMU and beyond and, in conjunction with the European and national statistical offices, would regularly, e.g. monthly and quarterly, publish independent reports on the fiscal positions of *all* EMU nations. Unlike current propositions, no individual nation would be singled out, but of course those in crisis would be focused upon. Council reports would of course always have to account for trends in national wage levels and competitiveness, which are usually subsequently reflected in government fiscal positions (Sheets and Sockin, 2012b). These regular independent Council reports would be a counterweight to the inherent inertial tendency of governments and bureaucracies to employ rules of thumb to entrench explosive incremental behaviour to their detriment until, from time to time, a breaking point is reached (see Dempster and Wildavsky, 1982, and the references therein).

To ensure minimal political interference with the new Council, a tall order with the current heterogeneous composition of EMU, the Council should be *independent* of the EU Commission and should report formally to the democratically elected Council of Finance Ministers. It should also set up a quarterly reporting schedule with press conferences so that there is *transparency* in its monitoring of EMU nations' fiscal positions. As with the UK OBR, it can produce its own economic forecasts and may develop its own methodologies for judging the fiscal stance of nation states. An EMU incarnation of the OBR may in the first instance have the assistance of the OECD and the IMF in setting up monitoring responsibilities, seconding staff and in developing appropriate modelling methodologies.

The new Council should have a role in evaluating the currently proposed mechanisms for fiscal transfer. These range from mutually backed project bonds, through the mutual issuance of Eurobonds by the EMU to ultimately supplant national sovereign bond issuance, to a full fiscal transfer mechanism in the image of the US. (It has recently been observed that Arkansas is America's Greece.)

However, we favour a simple fiscal mechanism to stabilise unstable EMU nations: surplus nations through the proposed European Stability Fund (ESF), rather than the ECB (for which it is an inappropriate central bank role) should effect any direct buying of the debt of deficit nations.

3.5 European Sovereign Bankruptcy Court establishment

The principle of *independence* applied to the European Fiscal Council is required a *fortiori* for our recommendation of setting up an EU-wide European Sovereign Bankruptcy Court to preside in future over the negotiated fiscal and financial resolution of nations in difficulty. For the EU legislative process setting up this court, the principal point is to enact a sovereign version of the US Chapter 11, which would allow each sovereign in difficulty to stay creditors while working out an appropriate solution, using intergovernmental (EMU and IMF), and if possible global market, sources of funding and debt haircuts as appropriate. Good practice for nations potentially seeking the Court's protection would be to work out as much of a plan for crisis resolution with the relevant institutions beforehand.

The Court should be set up as a subsidiary of the European Court of Justice, as an arm of the EU judiciary, independent of the EU Commission, Parliament and Council of Ministers. However, unlike its appeals superior, which would remain as is, i.e. with equal national justice representation, the new court would have *population proportional* national justice representation to maximise expertise and minimise corruption. The experience of the new Dutch government-sponsored International Financial Court in The Hague may be relevant in setting up the new Bankruptcy Court. We envision a panel of judges for each case, say three, one each from a large, medium and small country, but with the decision of the Chairman to be definitive. All private, EMU and IMF representations would be considered by the panel in coming to a deliberation, which would be final and announced over a weekend when global financial markets are closed.

The new court could be applied to by Greece, currently the most likely (temporary) leaver of EMU. The Court is complementary to the proposed European Fiscal Council, whose role would be to help it establish and monitor the ongoing fiscal components of its agreements.

In the long run this court would have many of the effects that the Germans currently seek, but without the already dire short-term consequences. In this regard it is interesting to note that from the beginning basic bankruptcy law was enshrined in the US constitution.

Current EU bankruptcy law at all levels is in disarray and also requires EMU and EU state attention. Somewhat more co-operation and co-ordination in this area could eventually lead to more innovative and dynamic national economies.

3.6 Summary of recommendations

The four recommendations above: European Central Bank and TARGET2 system reform, banning Tobashi swaps and short-term net uncovered positions in CDS on sovereign debt, and establishing both a European Fiscal Council and a European Sovereign Bankruptcy Court, should be implemented as soon as possible. Beginning on this path immediately, while not without its opponents, is (just) politically feasible. It is likely ultimately to be accepted by the global capital markets and so calm them.

CHAPTER 4
MONETARY ARRANGEMENTS

4.1 Late 20th century solutions to credible commitment

IN ORDER to provide a credible commitment, the Euro was established with no exit routes. This element of policy design was influenced by (i) the incomplete internal adjustment that characterised the ERM of the European Monetary System, and a host of fixed but adjustable pegs during the post-war Bretton Woods period, and (ii) the regular need for devaluations and speculative attacks that characterised exchange rate regimes in which the requirements of the external nominal exchange rate was in conflict with the requirements of internal stability. The commitment to the Euro involved the irrevocable locking of exchange rates and abandonment of national currencies. In principle this would not necessarily be problematic for adjustment to shocks if there were to be sufficient wage and price flexibility, labour mobility and a system of fiscal transfers from creditor to debtor nations. The ECB would then offer an institutional device, free of political influence, which could pursue aggregate price stability. Ultimately, the credibility that comes from being a locked-up member of monetary union is limited to a judgement about whether the gains from exit actually outweigh the gains from remaining with the monetary union

– if a widespread belief develops that the former gain domi-
nates, the credibility of the union will be threatened and so
some kind of option to exit will be valued by all participants.
A decade or so in, it would appear that this monetary union,
as so many previously, does actually require an escape route.

4.2   Escape routes and exit clauses

Chadha and Hudson (1997) catalogue the experience of several
monetary unions. The 'Gold Standard' was one monetary
union which permitted substantial membership flexibility.
Bordo and Schwartz (1994) catalogue the almost revolving
door nature of the gold standard for 21 core and periphery
countries. One explanation for the flexibility, put forward by
Bordo and Kydland (1990) and others, lies with the credibility
of the commitment technology. A country's commitment to
the Gold Standard was contingent: a country suffering from an
asymmetric shock could leave the system and, having pursued
a corrective policy, could return at its old parity. Alternatively,
it could face higher borrowing costs by seeking a devaluation.
The usual problem with such flexibility, for example under
Bretton Woods, is that other nations would also tend to seek
a competitive devaluation. But here the fact that a country
had to leave the system first, and could only re-access international capital upon its return, would increase the costs of
any use of this contingent mechanism and hence reinforce the
credibility of the system. Some Latin American countries, for
example, were 'off' as often as they were 'on'. Yet other countries – France, Germany, the USA and the UK – seem to have
operated the Gold Standard *almost* without break.

So if it was so flexible, why did the Gold Standard break
down? The Standard ultimately failed as a result of a complex
set of economic (and political) factors: the ending of Britain's
clear commitment to the Standard undermined a key deter-
minant of other countries adherence; and in the 1920s and

1930s countries began to believe that persistent real benefits could accrue from devaluation and declining international co-operation coincided with the growing difficulties of operating the fixed exchange rate system; and different experiences of adjustment in the 1920s and the development of wage and price rigidities made the use of independent monetary policy more attractive – particularly in a regime of greater political instability and consequent budgetary difficulties.

A key early exiter from the Gold Standard was the Bank of England itself, which during the French Revolutionary Wars, suspended payment in cash (gold) for Bank of England notes. This measure was adopted temporarily with the approval of the King, Privy Council, City of London merchants and the Prime Minister. The commitment to return to cash payments was renewed under a sequence of Acts of Parliament that tied the Government's hands once an enduring peace accord had been reached. Following exit in 1797, the Bank of England re-adopted payments in gold of its note issuance de facto in 1819 and returned to cash payment at the previous rate of exchange between sterling and gold. A wide range of factors explain the success of this temporary suspension of the Gold Standard, but maintaining a transparent approach to the question of return, through numerous Parliamentary Committees and reinforcement of the intention with legislation, played a key role. [4]

4.3 Historical currency break-ups

In practice, what constitutes a currency or monetary unions versus a separate currency is not clear-cut. At its most extreme a monetary union should constitute a single currency with a single central bank. A more flexible definition allows for a fixed exchange rate with convertibility. This fixed rate may be absolute and irrevocable or, at the other end of the spectrum, allow

---

4   See Chadha and Newby (2010) for more details on this exit policy.

limited levels of fluctuations (as under the Gold Standard). Rose (2007) uses the loosest definition of monetary union in his survey produces a sample of 69 break-ups since 1945 and concluded that:

> "In general, there are remarkably few signs of dramatic macroeconomic events either preceding or following currency union dissolutions."[5]

This view has been influential in creating a perception that currency union break-ups are not associated with macro-economic volatility.

We do not believe that this correctly summarises the empirical evidence. Rose classifies New Zealand switching from the New Zealand Pound to the New Zealand Dollar in July 1967 as a currency union break-up. However, the New Zealand pound had been a distinct currency since 1933, when New Zealand coinage was introduced. Even prior to 1933, bank notes were issued by private trading banks, although British and Australian coinage did circulate in New Zealand. This meant that there could be only small divergences between New Zealand and British Pounds. With the break-down in the Gold Standard in the summer of 1931 the New Zealand pound was able to depreciate not only against gold, but also against sterling, with GBP:NZP trading at around 1.25.

There are some other errors in Rose's survey (e.g. the EACB broke up in1966 not 1978, with separate currencies from 1966 onwards, albeit at a relatively stable exchange rate). Adjusting for these errors shows that the majority of events in his sample are currency exchange rate regime changes that occurred either during the Bretton Woods period or in the aftermath of the suspension of convertibility of the USD in 1971. Furthermore, separate currencies circulated in the majority of the unions, making the act of break-up considerably more complex.

---

5   "Checking Out: Exits from Currency Unions". MAS Staff Paper No.44, April 2007.

In this subsection we broaden the time horizon, but restrict our analysis to currency unions and break-ups where there was a higher degree of monetary integration. In particular, we examine examples where either there was a single currency circulating throughout the union or, although different currencies were issued, there was free circulation of these currencies between the differing regions. We therefore differ from Chadha and Hudson (1997) in excluding the Gold Standard in our sample, but rather recognise that the Gold Standard was an important building block to the British-Irish and Scandinavian monetary unions. The Silver Standard similarly had a role in the development of the English-Scottish, United States, and Latin monetary unions.

An exhaustive list of every monetary unions would involve surveying the formation (and break-downs) of all sovereign states. We instead focus on monetary unions between entities which had been independent sovereign states before the breakdown, at least until recently. We examine six monetary unions that are still in existence and a further six historical monetary unions which have broken up.

Currency unions still in existence today

England-Scotland (1707)

Monetary union was a component of the Act of Union of 1707 which formed the United Kingdom. The union between England and Scotland in 1707 involved irrevocably fixing the exchange rate between the nations with 12 pounds Scots equal to one pound Sterling. As with the later developments of the US dollar and the German thaler, a single currency was an important component of the nation-building process, reducing distinctions between the two areas and enhancing trade. The Anglo-Scottish union was asymmetric. There was no Scottish central bank comparable to the Bank of England and, although the three largest clearing banks had the right to print currency, their seigniorage rights were relatively limited, with the majority of currency issuance having to be backed with reserves at the Bank of England.

With the increasing popular support of the Scottish National Party and its majority in the Scottish Parliament since May 2011, the question of Scotland's continued membership of this monetary union has gained more prominence. A break-up would entail either using a new pounds Scot, continuing with Sterling or joining the Eurozone, as advocated in the 2009 SNP manifesto.

US Monetary Union (1781)

From the Colonial period until 1873 the US largely operated a bi-metallic standard before moving to the Gold Standard. The Bank of North America, chartered in 1781, operated as the United States' first central bank (see Wilson, 1942). This was followed by the First (chartered 1791) and Second (chartered 1816) Banks of the United States which operated as central banks until their charters expired after 20 years. Between 1838 until 1863 a free banking system operated with notes issued by hundreds of banks. With the passing of the National Bank Act in 1863, a unified currency was introduced and new national banks were allowed to issue notes only to the extent that they were backed by Federal bonds. Taxes on State bank note issuance eventually suppressed issuance by State banks. However, central banking and a uniform currency did not become well-established in the US until 1913 when the Federal Reserve System was created.

German Monetary Union I (1837)

The exact timing of German Monetary Union is open to some debate. Holtfrerirch (1993) argues that monetary union had effectively taken place long before political union in 1871, with the Munich Coin Treaty of 1837 creating a currency union in the southern German states, followed in 1838 by one for the

German customs union ('The Zollverein') as a whole with the Dresden Coin Convention. Restrictions on individual states issuance of small-change coins and fixed exchange rates led to the Prussian thaler becoming the dominant coin. Holtfrerirch argues that the use of the Silver Standard 'depoliticised money' and enabled monetary union.

Belgium-Luxembourg Economic Union (1839)

Although BLEU was born out of the break-up of the Latin Monetary Union (LMU – see below), Belgium and Luxembourg had been sharing a common currency since 1839, when Luxembourg gained independence from the Netherlands. An exception was the period 1842 to 1848 when the Prussian thaler was used in Luxemburg. Once the LMU had effectively broken up, the link with Belgium was largely based on the gold standard, so when Belgium devalued against gold in 1935, Luxembourg did not follow suit. Mommen (1994) argues that Belgian banks had been suffering from an outflow of deposits, which turned into a run over February and early March 1935. Capital controls were introduced on 18th March, 12 days before the currency was depreciated by 28% against gold. Sufficiently differentiated coinage and notes meant this process was relatively smooth. The experience of Belgium, as a country suffering from the Great Depression was not significantly different from others on the Gold Standard. The parity against gold, rather than its exchange rate against a small neighbour, was clearly more important in determining its competitiveness. Speculating against a change in parity was already relatively easy and membership of BLEU was not crucial to this process. After 1944 the parity was restored, with both currencies being legal tender in each area. This remained the case until the issuance of the euro in 2002.

German Monetary Union II: Western and Eastern Germany (1990)

GMU2 occurred between the old GDR and the DRG. Deposits were converted at a 1:1 rate for a limited amount of assets per person, dependent on age. Assets held by non-residents accrued after 1989 were converted on a 3 to 1 basis. All other assets and debts were converted at a rate of 2 to 1. The average conversion rate was about 1.7:1. The second German monetary union was accompanied by massive fiscal transfers from West to East Germany.

West African and Central African CFA Franc zones (1945)

The West African and Central African CFA Francs are two separate currency unions which have themselves been tied to first the French Franc and then, since 1999, the Euro. Each has its own separate central bank, although there is a degree of common circulation.

Currency unions which have subsequently broken up

Irish-British Monetary Union (1701-1979)

The break-up of the Irish-Sterling Monetary Union in 1979, which started in 1701, offers an example of an orderly break-up. In 1826 a fixed exchange rate of 13 Irish pounds equal to 12 pounds sterling was set within the UK. As the Irish Free State from 1922, Ireland subsequently operated an exchange rate peg against sterling until 30th March 1979. Ireland then decided to enter the ERM, which the UK had opted out of. The anticipated depreciation of the IEP (Irish pound) did not lead to large scale capital outflows since Ireland had already imposed tight exchange rate controls prior to the shift in regime. Ireland was also fortunate in that the move occurred before sterling's rapid appreciation began in the early 1980s as a result of the discovery of North Sea oil. The rapid depreciation against sterling over 1981 undoubtedly contributed to an acceleration of inflation in Eire to an average of 20.2% in 1981. However, growth remained robust at 2.9% in 1980 and 2.5% in 1981 and the GBP: IEP exchange rate remained stable (see Figure 13).

Figure 13: British pound to Irish pound effective
         exchange rate 1978-2011

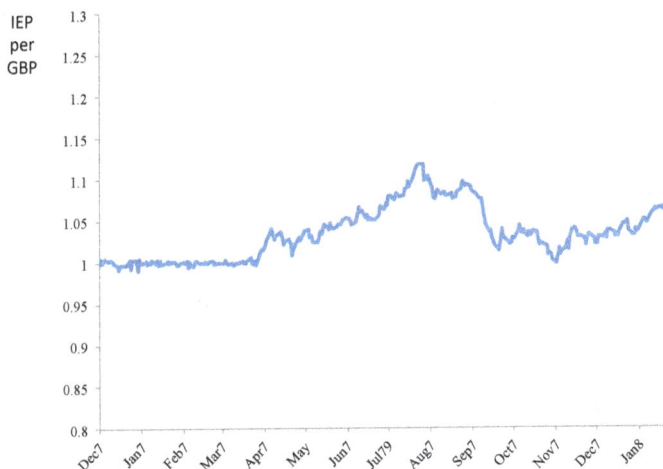

Source: Bloomberg and authors' calculations

Latin Monetary Union (1865–1927)

The Latin Monetary Union was primarily between France, Belgium, Italy and Switzerland. Although widely termed a currency union, the nations separately issued coinage from 1865. By implementing common standards it was hoped that the coins would be acceptable throughout the Union and this would boost trade. The coins contained 4.5g of silver or 1/15.5 of this weight in gold (free conversion was suspended in 1874). Although the union continued until the First World War (and was finally legally disbanded in 1927), both the Holy See and Greece were ejected for currency debasement (i.e. issuing silver coins with less silver than prescribed) much earlier, in the 19th century.

Austro-Hungarian Monetary Union (1867–1919)

The Austro-Hungarian Empire emerged from the Compromise of 1867 which merged the Hapsburg and Hungarian empires. This agreement created a monetary and customs union but kept distinct administrative regions. Initially there were two central banks, which were merged into 1878 to form the Austro-Hungarian bank, with 70% of note issuance by the Viennese branch and 30% by the Budapest branch, with the governments' shares of profits distributed equivalently (see Garber and Spencer, 1994). In 1892 the bank moved towards a gold standard with de facto convertibility. The onset of the first world war in 1914 suspended convertibility and saw the use of deficit financing to cover the cost of the war effort. Notes in circulation rose nearly 15-fold. With deficit financing continuing after the war, the various components of the former empire sought to move away from the old Austrian-Hungarian crowns. In a process mirrored to varying degrees of success throughout the former monetary area, movements of notes in and out of Czechoslovakia were prohibited from 25th February to March 9th 1919. Notes and bank deposits were converted into new crowns at a 1 for 1 exchange, with notes being over-stamped. However, 50% of funds were kept back and instead a non-tradable, non-redeemable 'bond' was issued for the balance. This was effectively an advance on a wealth tax that was to be later implemented. This wealth tax was also applied to bank deposits. One financial asset class to escape this tax was equities, which Garber and Spencer claim appreciated strongly despite the economic disruption. Hungary was the last successor state of the empire to issue a new currency.

Scandinavian Monetary Union (1873–1914)

The Scandinavian Monetary Union was formed in 1873 between Denmark and Sweden with their currencies, the rigsdale and the riksdaler, fixed against 0.403g of gold. Although there was some circulation within Scandinavia, these countries issued their own currencies. Sweden came off the Gold Standard in August 1914, which ended the monetary union.

Czech-Slovak Monetary Union (1919–1993)

Initially this union directly followed on from the break-up of the Austro-Hungarian monetary union.

More recently, Czechoslovakia's break-up into the Czech and Slovak Republics in 1993 was relatively successful. Over-stamping was used to introduce two separate currencies.

An expectation of appreciation of the Czech crown relative to the Slovak crown led to capital flight into the Czech Republic. Both currencies were introduced at par. Although the Slovakian crown depreciated, it was able to maintain stability against the Czech crown. In many respects the contrasts between Germany and Greece today are extreme versions of the contrasts between Slovakia and the Czech Republic in 1993. Both the Czech Republic in 1993 and Germany in 2009 had a revealed comparative advantage in high value added industries which typically have SITC7 codes (see Tables 3, 4 and 5).

Table 3: Greece's SITC export break-down 2010

SITC	Category	2010 $m	Avg.Growth Rates		2010 share
			2006-2010	2009-2010	
Total		21,559.7	0.7%	7.5%	100.0%
0+1	Food & animals + Beverages & Tobacco	4,765.6	7.5%	3.3%	22.1%
2+4	Crude Materials excl. Fuels + Animal & Veg. Oils	16,39.3	-4.1%	18.0%	7.6%
3	Mineral Fuels & Related	2,377.1	-3.4%	25.3%	11.0%
5	Chemicals	3,132.1	3.4%	7.5%	14.5%
6	Mfgd. Goods	4,319.4	0.2%	9.7%	20.0%
7	Machinery & Transport Equip.	2,578.8	-0.5%	-5.2%	12.0%
8	Misc. Mfgd. Articles	2,143.6	-3.5%		9.9%
9	Others	603.7	1.5%	57.8%	2.8%

Source: UN Comtrade (2011)

Table 4: Germany's SITC breakdown 2010

SITC Category		2010 $m	Avg. Growth Rates		2010 share
			2006-2010	2009-2010	
Total		1,271,096.3	3.2%	12.7%	100.0%
0+1	Food & animals + Beverages & Tobacco	62,919.7	7.5%	3.6%	5.0%
2+4	Crude Materials excl. Fuels + Animal & Veg. Oils	25,908.6	5.0%	33.5%	2.0%
3	Mineral Fuels & Related	23,907.1	-4.2%	3.3%	1.9%
5	Chemicals	187,399.5	4.5%	8.9%	14.7%
6	Mfgd. Goods	165,286.0	0.6%	14.4%	13.0%
7	Machinery & Transport Equip.	584,810.1	1.5%	16.5%	46.0%
8	Misc. Mfgd. Articles	128,974.5	4.1%	8.4%	10.1%
9	Others	91,890.8	18.6%	5.6%	7.2%

Source: UN Comtrade (2011)

As within Europe today, in Czechoslovakia there were significant barriers to labour mobility. Unemployment in the Czech Republic was 2.6% and 10.4% in Slovakia. Similarly, in Germany today the unemployment rate 6.9% versus 17.5% in Greece. The differences in unemployment rates suggested that there were already high barriers to labour mobility prior to break-up.

Following elections in June 1992, the Czech and Slovak republics decided to dismantle the federation from 1st of January 1993. It was agreed to maintain a common currency, a customs union, and to allow free movement of labour between the two countries (Rupnik and Zielonka, 2003). From late 1992 Slovak households and firms transferred deposits into Czech commercial banks. The central bank of Czechoslovakia had to increasingly fund Slovak banks (see Prokop, 1994) raising additional questions about the stability of the monetary union once the central bank was to break into its two constituent banks.

Table 5: Czech and Slovak SITC breakdown 1993

Category	Category	Czech Republic		Slovakia	
		Exports	Imports	Imports	Exports
SITC0	Food & animals	6.5%	6.3%	5.5%	7.3%
SITC1	Beverages & Tobacco	1.2%	1.1%	0.9%	1.5%
SITC2	Crude Materials excl. Fuels	6.1%	5.0%	4.9%	5.2%
SITC3	Mineral Fuels & Related	6.2%	11.1%	4.9%	20.9%
SITC4	Animal & Vegetable Oils	0.2%	0.4%	0.1%	0.2%
SITC5	Chemicals	9.5%	12.1%	12.0%	11.4%
SITC6	Mfgd. Goods	29.9%	15.9%	38.8%	15.1%
SITC7	Machinery & Transport Equip.	27.6%	36.1%	19.4%	29.3%
SITC8	Misc. Mfgd. Articles	12.7%	11.7%	13.4%	9.0%
SITC9	Others	0.0%	0.4%	0.1%	0.2%

Source: Fidrmuc and Horvath (1998)

Fidrmuc and Horvath (1998) argue that the overall economic impact was limited. GDP declined by 1% in the Czech Republic and 4% in Slovakia, with both countries rebounding in 1994. Continuous exchange rate data immediately after the break-up is not available. Dedek (1996) and Fidrmuc and Horvath (1998) both put the depreciation at 10%. An implied exchange rate using the crosses against the USD can be derived from Bloomberg data from late 1993. Prices used are mid-close prices and given the lack of liquidity, in the Slovak quote in particular, introduce a degree of negative serial correlation in the innovations to the cross rate. Ignoring the shorter terms fluctuations, it is clear that the Czech-Slovak cross exhibited a remarkable degree of stability (see Figure 14).

Figure 14: Slovak crown to Czech crown exchange rate 1993-2011

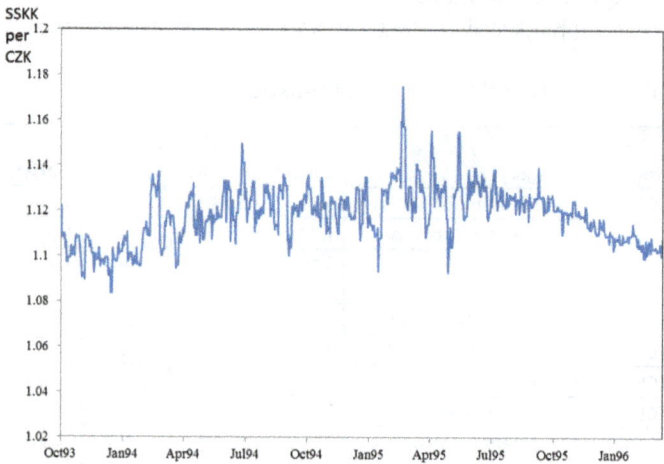

Source: Bloomberg and authors' calculations

Former USSR (1991–1993)

The break-up of the USSR led to a temporary monetary union with independent states over 1991 to 1993. Although only the Bank of Russia, the successor to the Gosbank, had the power to issue bank notes, all 15 of the new central banks of the former republics were able to issue credit to their banking systems. The period was characterised by hyper-inflation, since central banks were incentivised to extend as much credit as possible in order to free-ride on other central banks. Successor currencies typically had difficulty establishing credibility and also suffered from inflation. The exception was Estonia, which introduced a new currency, the kroon, under a currency board system pegged to the Deutschemark. Only a small number of roubles per person were allowed to be converted into the kroon, effectively creating a per capita allowance of the new currency.

Argentine Currency Board (1991–2002)

Argentina's currency board established a one-to-one peg against the US dollar with complete convertibility. However, relatively high inflation, unfavourable terms of trade shocks and poor productivity performance of Argentina had led to clear overvaluation of the Peso by 2001. Capital flight created a liquidity crisis for the banks and resulted in the introduction of 'la corralito' in December 2001. Under the 'corralito' households had all their accounts frozen and were unable to withdraw more than 250 pesos per week, with withdrawals from foreign currency accounts having to be converted into pesos. This was followed by 'la corralon' in which dollar assets were converted into pesos and additional capital controls were imposed. The currency board had encouraged the dollarisation of contracts. The government redominated these contracts through 'pesofisation'.

Break-up implications

Figure 15 shows for specific break-ups the fall in GDP occurring with currency depreciation within one year after the break-up event. The message of this plot is clear: for nations which found themselves in difficult situations prior to the break-up, in each case GDP – and hence national welfare – suffered significant drops. The implications for peripheral EMU members currently themselves under stress are that the consequences of exiting EMU and re-establishing their own currencies may be *extremely* severe.

Figure 15: New currency depreciations and GDP drops following break-ups

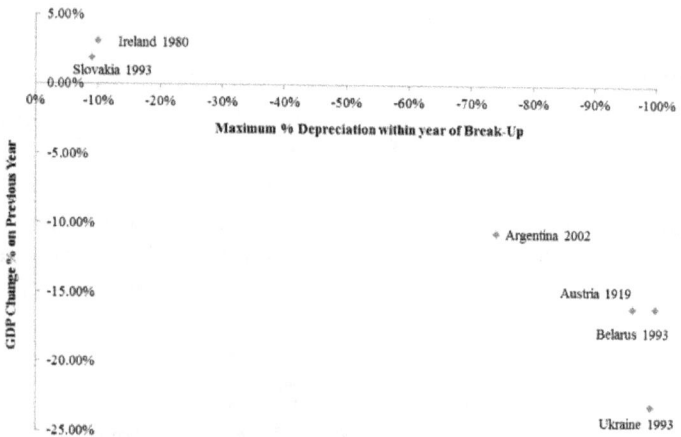

Source: Bloomberg, Maddison (2010), Garber & Spencer (1994)

On the other hand, if Germany were to leave the EMU and reintroduce the deutschmark, the likely rapid appreciation of the new 'safe haven' currency could possibly restore the nation's 1990's status as the 'sick man' of Europe.

4.4 Eurozone break-up issues

Break-ups of monetary unions or currency boards histori-cally have either meant a junior partner breaking away from a central bank or a relatively minor currency splitting off, often following the break-up of a sovereign state. A break-up of the Eurozone would represent a unique set of issues.

Firstly, the Euro is today the second most important currency in world financial markets and is extensively referenced by contracts and used by non-Eurozone residents. Secondly, the sovereignty of a country is best not considered as being binary, but lying on a spectrum of degrees of sovereignty (Nagan and Hammer, 2003). Members of the EU, in particular, have given up varying degrees of sovereignty to the institutions that make up the EU. 'Lex Monetae', the principle that sovereign countries are able to determine the legal tender used to settle transactions governed by their domestic law, is complicated if it is not clear whether a contract is governed by their particular national law or European law (Scott, 1998). From a European law perspec-tive, exit would therefore require treaty change and might mean EU exit. There are however a range of legal scenarios whereby a country can leave the EMU under Article 50 or, should it be 'asked to leave' under a solidarity principle, whereby it can impose significant costs on the others. Under our reset option described below we consider that some form of Article 50 could be invoked to induce a temporary national exit.

Remaining in the EU but leaving EMU

It is by no means clear whether a country could do this *unilat-erally*, since it would involve denunciation of some, but not all, treaties. However, attempts to do so would certainly lead to legal challenges to any attempts to redenominate contracts and is likely lead to a huge rise in transaction costs. Even if not theo-retically impossible, we believe that the legal uncertainty that this would create makes it *practically* impossible. A *negotiated* withdrawal from EMU, but not the EU, is therefore the only practical way of achieving this outcome. Treaty amendment can either be by an 'ordinary procedure' or a 'simplified' one. Under the ordinary procedure the European Council organises either a convention of parliaments or a conference of member states to negotiate treaty amendments. These then have to be ratified by all member states in accordance with their constitutions. Alternatively, treaties relating to the provisions on the Euro can also be amended by the 'simplified revision procedure', which only requires the Council of Ministers to adopt amendments by unanimity after consulting the EU Parliament and Commission.

Leaving both the EU and EMU

Article 50 of the Lisbon Treaty specifically provides for negotiated exit of the EU. However, even prior to the Lisbon Treaty unilateral exit was generally acknowledged to be possible. Leaving the EU without at least being able to negotiate remaining in the broader customs union (the European Free Trade Association, or EFTA) is likely to be a inefficient outcome. However, remaining in EFTA does represent an important option and bargaining chip for countries seeking to exit.

4.5 The reset option

The reset option for EMU could possibly be designed in one of two ways – internal wage and price adjustment or exchange rate devaluation. Debt forgiveness and heightened fiscal surveillance would operate in both cases.

In the first case, a country could leave EMU for a limited short period only, perhaps a week or a month, during which time it would reduce domestic wages and prices sufficiently to engineer an internal reset of the price level in order to regain competitiveness within the Eurozone. At the end of this rapid and time limited adjustment period, the country would rejoin the Eurozone.

There are two problems with such an option. How to set the appropriate internal devaluation of all wages and prices to deal not only with the historic degree of misalignment in the real exchange rate, but also to leave the domestic economy that has exercised the option with a real exchange rate that is closest to establishing internal and external equilibrium? In our view there is a considerable degree of uncertainty over any point estimate of the appropriate real exchange rate, as well as over how the country should adjust to the new monetary-fiscal settlement. The second problem is that it is simply not clear that weak governments will be able to deliver the required domestic price adjustments rapidly, as these will require considerable political will and co-operation across many elements of society – witness current Greek and Spanish government protestations. It is simply much easier and quicker to change an externally overvalued real exchange rate through devaluation against trading partners than it is to set appropriate domestic wage and price adjustments.

In the case of exchange rate devaluation, like the UK under the Gold Standard, a country would leave the Eurozone with the explicit intention of returning and the extended exit would allow an *external* adjustment of its competitive position upon the reintroduction of its domestic currency. The first step would be to develop the reset option with a postulated single leaver of EMU, e.g. Greece, which is only in the process of leaving, so that given speedy legislation and proper policy its situation is reversible. It would be much cheaper and much less disruptive to maintain EMU as it currently exists, assuming that the developments recommended in the previous section and below are in place. Compared to even recent history – the past 20 years – things are not as dire as they are currently made out to be (Childs, 2012), e.g. *net* Spanish corporate sector debt is currently *negative* and Italy has higher ratio of *private* wealth to GDP than other EMU nations, including Germany. The reset option would give such countries a breathing space.

The problem otherwise is one of different levels and dynamics of sovereign debt for most nations that are members of EMU. They also entered the Union at optimistic fixed currency exchange rates with the euro and subsequently enjoyed heterogeneously diverse productivity rates. Recently, relative to each nation's notional sustainable level of debt, their debt levels have altered drastically as a result of the policy measures taken to prop up national and domestic global banks – many in worse shape than was initially apparent to the market – in order to avoid national financial system collapse.

Thus to minimise the effects of a Euro crisis leading to the collapse of the Euro, three areas must be addressed: sovereign debt, effective exchange rates (leading to more convergence over the very long run) and financial sector soundness. Assuming that the latter can be adequately addressed over time by national governments achieving appropriate debt levels and with ESF and ECB, and likely IMF, support, this leaves only two areas to address. If all nations are to remain within EMU, including the leaver which will return, we argue that debt levels must be addressed initially and periodically through the proposed new EMU institutions and the concomitant result will be effective exchange rate adjustment to enhance national productivity and employment levels.

The Salter-Swan stylised analysis of fixed exchange rate zones plots *external* equilibrium (EE), with required real exchange rate as a negative function of *domestic* demand, termed *absorption*, versus internal equilibrium (IE), with the required real exchange rate a positive function of absorption (Figure 16). The full internal-external equilibrium represented by the intersection of the two curves in the figure corresponds to a real exchange rate which *exactly* balances external equilibrium and domestic demand at the fixed exchange rate.

Actually, this ideal equilibrium is of course subject to unexpected shocks, but in a Mundell optimal currency area these are relatively easily reversible by appropriate policy. In a fixed exchange rate area, on the other hand, countries with excessive levels of absorption relative to their productive capacity levels are likely to suffer from external payments deficits, and if their real exchange rate is too high, also from unemployment. It is these nations, with Greece first, that we judge could benefit from the development of the reset option. Obviously the creditor nations in EMU lie to the left of the EE curve in the figure. Overall, the deficits must be somehow balanced by the debtor nations, but when the scale of one country's debt overhang is sufficiently large to prevent adjustment, some form of debt restructuring will necessarily be required.

We propose that the sovereign debt level of all nations in EMU can be assessed by the Fiscal Council and if a specific nation's is deemed to be excessive, that country can apply for the reset option via the Sovereign Bankruptcy Court. The extent of the debt adjustment and external exchange rate adjustment can be implemented under the recommendation of the new EMU institutions, together with the market, EMU and the IMF. When an appropriate haircut of the current sovereign debt level of a nation has been negotiated through these institutions, the nation exits EMU at the old level and undergoes an extended period of adjustment and heightened monitoring until it re-enters EMU, at possibly a new level, say over a weekend while the markets are closed. All domestic and foreign obligations remain in place at the agreed reduced levels, but at the new national government debt levels the nation is in a position in the interim to ease the pain of all investors by appropriate fiscal policy specific to the situation at hand.

Figure 16: Salter-Swan, EMU and the reset option

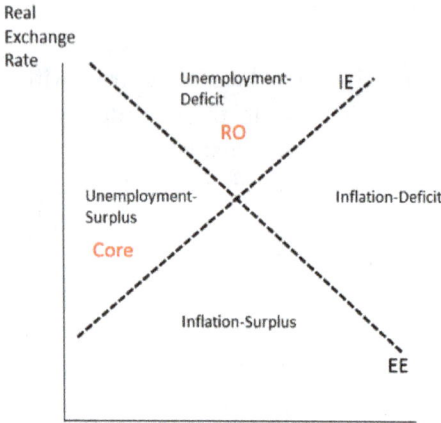

4.6 Introducing a new currency

The introduction of a new currency raises significant issues with regard to the practicality of speedy implementation and sequencing of reforms. Even in successful currency break-ups a degree of capital flight, in particular deposit flight, is unavoidable. However, quite a lot of the most 'unsticky' money is likely to have already left Greece, Spain and Italy, so we should not overstate the problem. In implementing the reset option, effective exchange rate and capital controls would need to be put into place as quickly as possible. For practicality, transactions outside the departing country would need to be suspended on announcement, as would large cash withdrawals from banks and movements of cash to outside the country. An extended bank holiday would need to be introduced during this interim period. Given the extensive use of ATMs and a greater use of electronic payment mechanisms, a pure currency stamping operation as has been employed historically would not now be practical. There would therefore need to be a period of around a month for ATM, bank system, and payment and settlement system reprogramming.

CHAPTER 5

CONCLUSION

THE EFFERVESCENCE of the early years of the EMU project (see, for example, the self-congratulatory *The Euro at Ten*, ECB, 2009,) has been replaced with a form of trench warfare: markets, central banks, Brussels and the IMF seem resigned to each yard or so of progress at great cost. Rather than breaking up the Eurozone, we want to break up the *problem* and we suggest that policy-makers not only concentrate on the necessary reforms for a currency union but also offer to put the victims of the battle into intensive care.

We therefore think that any suggested solution to the EMU crisis ought to meet the following necessary criteria:

(i) Allow the remaining core of EMU to continue as a hard currency zone;

(ii) Allow the problematic economies to be nursed back to health; and

(iii) Give these peripheral countries an option to return to EMU at some future point.

Solving the problems of EMU has proved very difficult and, as Palmerston said of another European problem on which traction was rather hard: "Only three people...have ever really understood the Schleswig-Holstein business –the Prince Consort, who is dead; a German professor, who has gone mad;

and I, who have forgotten all about it." The EMU problem offers a similar puzzle: how to manage a cessation that keeps the rest of the monetary union intact? In our view developing a reset option will maintain the stability of the core union, the peripheral union and the overall financial system and payment mechanism.

Any suggested solution to the problems of EMU is potentially second best. It must deal with an unfortunate starting point after the crisis and a dozen years of incomplete monetary integration. There are a number of possible gambits. One is to attempt to reform the whole system without developing any option for the reset discussed in this book. The argument runs that, by showing no willingness to tamper with the structure of EMU member-ship, the highest degree of internal adjustment can be imposed on peripheral members of the currency union, and that absent-ing a reset option is the best way to keep the EMU in existence. However, there are two arguments against this position which we find compelling. First, the development of an option to reset can be valuable, as it provides peripheral countries with a further alternative to the status quo or complete abandonment of EMU. Secondly, the reset option will allow policy reformers to work in the interim on the declared necessary reform of the extant monetary union as a parallel project.

Our solution is clear. Reform the core monetary union and offer the periphery an option to reset. The advantage to the core members is that their current systems of currency and payments can continue unabated. Necessary reform of the core can then be carried out without altering the fundamental rules for a monetary union. For example, in order to promote appro-priate fiscal policies across the extant union once the option has been exercised, there should be no purchases or monetary financing of fiscal deficits without the sanction of the new democratic institutions. In this way, the reset option offers the best way to guarantee the future prosperity of members of the EMU, and of the EU.

BIBLIOGRAPHY

Bank of England, Financial Stability Review, December 2011.

Buiter, W H, E Rahbari, and J Michels (2011), "The Implications of Intra-Euro Area Imbalances in Credit Flows", CEPR Policy Insight No. 57.

Buiter, W H, E Rahbari, and J Michels (2011), "Making Sense of Target Imbalances", September 2011. http://www.voxeu.org/index.php?q=node/6945

Bundesbank "Bundesbank target 2 balances", 22nd February 2011. http://www.bundesbank.de/download/presse/pressenoti-zen/2011/20110222.target2-salden.en.php?print=yes&

Chadha, J S, October 2010, Evidence to the House of Lords European Union Committee The Future of Governance in the EU.

Chadha, J S, 13th January 2012, Evidence to the Parliamentary Scrutiny Committee, Possibilities for Re-Enforcing the Eurozone Following the December European Council.

Chadha, J S and S. Hudson, 1997, A Short Survey of Monetary Unions, unpublished mimeo.

Chadha, J S and Newby, E., "Midas, transmuting all, into paper': the Bank of England and the Banque de France during the Napoleonic Wars", prepared for Chicago meeting of Economic History Association 2010.

Childs, B (2012), "Fate of the euro: A contrarian view", *International Herald Tribune*, 25th January 2012, 12.

Cohen, B (1993), "Beyond EMU: The Problem of Sustainability", *Economics and Politics*, 5, 187.

Dedek O (1996), "The Break-up of Czechoslovakia: an In-depth economic analysis" Aldershot, Avebury.

Dempster, M A H and A B Wildavsky (1982), "Modelling the US spending process: Overview and implications", in: R C O Matthews and G B Stafford, eds. *The Grants Economy and the Financing of Collective Consumption*, International Economics Association Proceedings, Macmillan, London, 267-309.

Dempster, M A H, E A Medova and J Roberts (2011). "Regulating complex derivatives: Can the opaque be made transparent?", *Journal of Banking Regulation*, 12(4), 308-330.

Di Cesare, A G Grande, M Manna and M Taboga (2012), Recent estimates of sovereign risk premia for euro-area countries, Banca D'Italia Working Paper 128.

Durre, A and F Smets (2012). "Sovereign debt and monetary policy in theory and practice: The case of the Euro area" forthcoming in *Macroeconomics and the Yield Curve – After the Financial Crisis*, Cambridge University Press, 2013.

ECB (2009), "Guideline of the European Central Bank", 7th May 2009.

ECB (2007), "Guideline of the European Central Bank", 26th April 2007.

ECB (2005), "Guideline of the European Central Bank", 30th December 2005.

ECB (2009), "The Euro at Ten – Lessons and Challenges", Fifth ECB Central Banking Conference, 13-14 November 2008.

European Union (2008), "Consolidated versions of the Treaty on European Union and the Treaty on the Functioning of the European Union", 9th May 2008.

European Union (1992), "Treaty on European Union", 29th July 1992.

European Union (1997), " Treaty of Amsterdam amending the Treaty on European Union, the Treaties establishing the European Communities and certain related acts", 10th November 1997.

Fidrmuc, J and J Horvath (1998), "Stability of Monetary Unions: Lessons from the Break-Up of Czechoslovakia," Discussion Paper 1998-74", Tilburg University, Center for Economic Research.

Garber, P and M Spencer (1994), "The Dissolution of the Austro-Hungarian Empire: Lessons for Currency Reform", No 191 Princeton Essays in International Finance.

Graeber, D (2011), *Debt: The First 5000 Years*, Melville House Publishing, New York.

Holtfrerich, C L (1993), "Did monetary unification precede or follow political unification of Germany in the 19th century", *European Economic Review*, 37, 518-524.

Maddison, A (2010). Website source: http://www.ggdc.net/maddison/.

Meyers, J and D Lewis (1998), "The introduction of the Euro: Overview of the legal framework and selected legal issues" Columbia Journal of European Law, 4, 321.

Mommen, A (1994), *The Belgian Economy in the Twentieth Century*. Routledge, London.

Mundell, R A (1961), "A theory of optimum currency wars", *American Economic Review*, 51(4), 657-665.

Nagan, W P and C Hammer (2004), "The Changing Character of Sovereignty in International Law and International Relations", *Columbia Journal of Transnational Law*, 43, 141.

Prokop, L (1994), "Priprava a prubeh menove odluky v Ceske republice v r. 1993", Czech National Bank Research Paper No. 28.

Reuters (9th December 2011), Breaking Views, Banks' Stress Tests, International Herald Tribune.

Rose, A (2007), "Checking out: Exits from currency unions", Monetary Authority of Singapore Staff Paper No. 44, April.

Rose, A (2008), "Currency unions", *New Palgrave Dictionary of Economics*, Second Edition, Palgrave Macmillan, London.

Rupnik, J and J Zielonka, eds, (2004), *The Road to the European Union. Vol. 1*: The Czech Republic and Slovakia. Manchester: Manchester University Press.

Scott, H S (1998), "When the Euro falls apart", *International Finance*, 1(2), 207-228.

Sheets, N and R A Sockin (2012a), "Empirical and thematic perspectives: Alexander Hamilton and Germany's "windfall" from Euro-area membership", Citi Investment Research and Analysis, Citigroup Capital Markets, New York, 17th January 2012.

Sheets, N and R A Sockin (2012b), "Empirical and thematic perspectives: Germany's "windfall" from Euro-area membership and European imbalances", Citi Investment Research and Analysis, Citigroup Capital Markets, New York, 27th January 2012.

Sinn, H W and T Wollmershaeuser (2011), "Target loans, current account balances and capital flows: The ECB's rescue facility", NBER Working Paper 17626.

Smithers, A (2011), "Germany's Self Interest and the Euro", Smithers & Co. Report 384, 23rd June.

Wallace, C P (2012), "Banking Crisis, Part II", *Fortune Magazine,* 15th January, 7.

Walters A A (1990), *Sterling in Danger: Economic Consequences of Fixed Exchange Rates*, Fontana Press, London.

Wilson, J, "The Bank of North America and Pennsylvania politics: 1781-1787," *Pennsylvania Magazine of History and Biography,* 46(1), The Historical Society of Pennsylvania, 3-28.

AUTHORS' BIOGRAPHIES

JAGJIT S CHADHA
Professor of Economics at the University of Kent and on the Advisory Board of the Centre of International Macroeconomics and Finance at the University of Cambridge. Previously Professor of Economics at the University of St Andrews and Fellow at Clare College, Cambridge, he was educated at University College London and the London School of Economics and then moved to the Bank of England as an Official working on Monetary Policy. He was Chief Quantitative Economist at BNP Paribas from 2005 to 2007 and is Series Editor of *Modern Macroeconomic Policy-Making* published by Cambridge University Press.

MICHAEL A H DEMPSTER
Professor Emeritus at the Centre for Financial Research, University of Cambridge. Educated at Toronto, Carnegie-Mellon and Oxford, he has taught and researched in major universities on both sides of the Atlantic and is founding Editor-in-Chief of *Quantitative Finance* and of the *Oxford Handbooks in Finance*. Consultant to many global financial institutions and governments, he is regularly involved in executive education worldwide. Author of over 120 research articles in leading international journals and 13 books, his work has won several awards and he is an Honorary Fellow of the UK Institute of Actuaries and Managing Director of Cambridge

Systems Associates Limited, a financial analytics consultancy and software company.

DERRY E PICKFORD

Macro-Analyst, Ashburton London, a division of FirstRand Bank Limited (London Branch). He was educated at Clare College, Cambridge. Previously Chief Economist for eight years at Sloane Robinson, an equity hedge fund manager, he spent three years as Economic Analyst at Smithers & Co., a macro-economic consultancy specialising in macro imbalances and their implications for financial markets. Whilst at Smithers he served on the EUROPA working group looking at best practice for financial market analysts and continues to work on how multiple principal-agent relationships acted to magnify noise in financial markets.

www.ingramcontent.com/pod-product-compliance
Lightning Source LLC
Chambersburg PA
CBHW071138280326
41935CB00010B/1278